Making Faith Fun

Making Faith Fun

132 spiritual activities
you can do with your kids

Amy Viets

acta
PUBLICATIONS

MAKING FAITH FUN
132 Spiritual Activities You Can Do with Your Kids
by Amy Viets

Edited by Marcia Broucek
Cover design by Tom A. Wright
Text Design and typesetting by Patricia Lynch

All Scripture quotations are from the *New Revised Standard Version Bible*,copyright ©
1989 by the Division of Christian Education of the National Council of the Churches of
Christ in the USA. Used by permission.

Copyright © 2006 by ACTA Publications,

Published by ACTA Publications, 5559 W. Howard Street, Skokie, IL 60077
(800) 397-2282 www.actapublications.com.

Library of Congress Number: 2006925717
ISBN 10: 0-87946-303-1
ISBN 13: 978-0-87946-303-8
Printed in the United States of America
Year: 15 14 13 12 10 9 8 7 6
Printing: 10 9 8 7 6 5 4 3 2

CONTENTS

To Bruce, Kayla, Layney and Garrett,
who have always believed in me
and given me the time and space to keep writing.

Introduction

Make purses for yourselves that do not wear out,
an unfailing treasure in heaven,
where no thief comes near and no moth destroys.
For where your treasure is, there your heart will be also.
—Luke 12:33-34

I t was a typical Sunday morning, our family of five stretching across most of one pew.

"Remember, I have to be back at church for band practice at 5:00 today," our thirteen-year-old daughter, Kayla, whispered in my ear.

"Mama, can you reach my quarter?" Garrett, our eight-year-old, asked. His offering has an unfortunate habit of rolling away right before the plate comes past.

My husband, Bruce, passed me a note. Really, he did—as if we were back in high school. "We need to mark the calendar with that change in Layney's gymnastics class." We'd both forgotten to take our ten-year-old daughter to gymnastics last week, and we didn't want to repeat that mistake.

While I had his note (actually the blank side of the Sunday bulletin) in hand, I grabbed a pen from my purse and scribbled a few other reminders: "E-mail Mom." "Pick up milk on the way home." "Make cookies for school." I kept writing. The list seemed endless.

It wasn't until I heard the pastor reading from the Gospel of Luke that my pen quit moving over the paper: "Make purses for yourselves that do not wear out, an unfailing treasure in heaven, where no thief comes near and no moth destroys. For where your treasure is, there your heart will be also."

I felt as if the Holy Spirit had come right up behind me, enveloped me in loving warmth and whispered in my ear, "Listen...this is for you."

I did listen. And I thought. And I prayed.

Bruce and I had always given God credit for the blessings of our family. But beyond mealtime and bedtime prayers, it didn't feel as if we were really living out our faith. How could we? We were trying to navigate work commitments, piano lessons, gymnastics, school concerts, church involvement. Let's face it, we had a lot going on. Hmm….

At least earthly treasure wasn't really that important to us, I thought. We didn't go overboard with material possessions. But there was no denying we did our share of whining about driving a sixteen-year-old car and never going on a "real" vacation. Hmm…

Hey, I told myself, we come to church together every Sunday—what more could anyone expect? My thoughts stopped as abruptly, as if the organist had bellowed out "Onward Christian Soldiers" when the congregation was expecting "On Eagle's Wings." I couldn't recall a single Bible verse that exhorted us to worship and glorify God only one day out of the week. In fact, I thought, squirming uncomfortably, I seemed to remember something in our liturgy about "at all times and in all places." Hmm….

All those "hmms" suddenly turned into one big "aha!" Our family had been so busy—running after things that don't last, things that wear out—that we'd put our hearts in the wrong place. In spite of our thankfulness for all God had given us, we weren't giving our best in return. We had become a "Sunday faith" family.

When Bruce and I managed to catch up with each other in the same room for a few minutes that afternoon, we talked this over and came up with a plan. Regular family devotions were the answer, we decided. Somewhere on one of our overcrowded bookshelves was a devotional the kids had brought home from Sunday School. After many dust-induced sneezes, I finally found it. I flipped through the bright, colorful pages. Fun pictures—good. Daily Bible readings—good. Discussion questions—good. Follow-up projects—good, if I could round up the supplies.

But, strangely, we were fresh out of toilet paper tubes, pipe cleaners and glitter, so I couldn't round up the supplies. In fact, I couldn't even round up my family. Kayla had to get to band practice. Garrett and Layney were glued to a movie. Bruce was in the middle of an auto repair project—with a sixteen-year-old car, we had a lot of those. Maybe we could gather for a family devotion tomorrow evening.

I checked the calendar. No, I had a meeting. Okay, Tuesday night. Nope, the school orchestra concert. Wednesday? Choir practice. How about Thursday? The calendar was clear for Thursday evening. We'd do it then.

But then I remembered those all-important words: "At all times and in all places." Not just on Sunday mornings. Not just when we're all planning to be home and we can manage to fit it in.

It was another "aha" moment. Limiting devotional time to some distant date when we could all get together wasn't a very worthy expression of our faith. What we needed was the living faith we spoke of in our liturgy at church. Instead of making our family fit into the traditional mold of devotion time, we needed to weave our faith into the mesh of our lives.

Armed with this revelation, I spent some time in bookstores and libraries looking for devotionals that would help us do just that. No luck. I found many well-written and faith-filled resources, but none of them seemed practical. Every family devotion I studied required preparation time, collection of craft supplies, and/or a specifically-defined, daily family meeting time.

At about the same time, I began hearing concerns similar to mine from other families at our church. As the Director of Children's Ministries, I am blessed with many opportunities to visit with parents about what's working and what's not in their family faith journey. Over and over again parents echoed my thoughts: They liked the ideas they saw in so many family devotionals, but they never got past the "hmm… that sounds like a nice idea" stage. Intimidated by the preparation and execution time required, they simply gave up.

Once again I felt the Holy Spirit's gentle whisper. If what we needed wasn't out there, maybe I was being asked to do something about it. I began to jot down (and try) some ideas for living our faith in the midst of our busy schedules and hectic lives, always keeping in mind what was practical and "do-able."

It was when Bruce and I played the "What If" game with Kayla, Layney and Garrett (see Chapter One, "On the Road") that we discovered the power of a new type of family devotion. What normally would have been idle time—kids wearing headphones, Bruce's eyes glued to the road, and my nose buried in a book—turned into a moment of living faith. With simple questions—such as, "What if everyone in your class were being mean to a new kid? How could God help you do the right thing?"—our kids became actively engaged and even begged for more questions. The responses they came up with were phenomenal in their depth. They were truly thinking over what they'd learned about faith and applying it to realistic situations. As I witnessed their enthusiasm for the game, the concept for *Making Faith Fun* began to take shape.

Making Faith Fun is divided into chapters that reflect the everyday routines of most families. You'll recognize the challenges and opportunities we all face, and you'll find simple, practical suggestions for turning busy moments into a living faith—no toilet paper tubes, pipe cleaners or glitter required.

I suggest starting with Chapter One, "Different Ages, Different Stages" for a brief review of the differing interests, abilities and challenges for children at various stages of growth. Then jump to a chapter that focuses on a daily routine you'd like to infuse with a healthy dose of living faith. Read through the chapter and try out a few of the suggested activities. I believe you'll be as excited as we were by the way your family faith life grows as a result.

I must admit our family is very lucky in that we're the typical, suburban, nuclear household. We feel privileged that day care has never been an issue for us: Since our oldest was born, either Bruce or I has been able to be a stay-at-home parent. But we've faced our share of challenges, including long-term illness and the resulting financial strain. We struggle with the same frustrations and shortcomings as anyone else, from peer pressure to new-car envy. I'm impatient and action-oriented, while Bruce is methodical and deliberate—an often volatile mix. Our three kids are so different in emotional make-up you'd never guess they share the same genes. In short, I'm convinced that if "living faith moments" can take place in our flawed yet very average family, they can happen for anyone.

Though our family has two parents, single parents are every bit as capable of creating a living, active faith within their families. Whatever the size or shape of your family, allow God to be your partner as you work to build that faith. Know that God is beside you, encouraging, comforting, and loving you through all you do.

Here are a few tips for *Making Faith Fun* work for your family:

- Don't be bound by the traditional concept of what a family devotion looks like. Take a chance on something new and different. For "the word of God is living and active" (Hebrews 4:12), just as our families are living and active.

- Don't beat yourself up based on an image of the "perfect family." Despite our best intentions, there will always come a time when we're too worn out to even consider how we might turn a busy day into a time of living faith. God knows, God understands, God loves, and God forgives. And we can get up the next day to try again, giving thanks to God for that grace.

- Though the ideas in each chapter are divided into age groups, be flexible. Don't toss out an idea just because it seems too childish. You might be surprised at what your fourth grader thinks is fun! After all, "unless you change and become like little children, you will never enter the kingdom of heaven" (Matthew 18:3). And don't forget that we as parents can have some fun too. We're only as old as we force ourselves to be.

The activities suggested in *Making Faith Fun* are for ordinary people, with full schedules and demanding days, and require no special training. Neither my husband nor I have been to seminary, and neither one of us is a Bible expert. But we have discovered that there is something about sharing our faith with our children in simple, everyday ways that deepens our relationship with God.

If your family hasn't had much practice talking about faith, it may be a little difficult to get started. I know we felt pretty awkward at first using God-language in the midst of our normal routine. But it got easier. At some point it even felt natural. And we knew that meant our family had learned to recognize and honor the presence of God at all times and in all places.

I pray that you will have the same experience. Many blessings to you and your family as you live your faith and discover where your treasure is.

—Amy Viets

CHAPTER ONE

Different Ages, Different Stages

God enters by a private door into every individual.
—Ralph Waldo Emerson

You are the number one expert on your children. Over the years you've learned what works—or doesn't work—with each of them. You may have discovered, as Bruce and I did, that your children can be so shockingly different from each other that you wonder whether someone was switched at birth. We are all, indeed, "fearfully and wonderfully made" (Psalm 139:14). Just because you're all related doesn't mean you all learn the same way, that you all have the same strengths, or that you all experience the presence of Christ in the same way. When you can celebrate these differences, you can discover amazing opportunities to strengthen your family's faith.

Though they are all blessedly unique, children do tend to show some similarities at certain stages of development. For the sake of the faith-building activities in each chapter, I've provided four age ranges: infant and toddler (up to age 3), preschool (ages 3 to 5), elementary (ages 5 to 10), and preteen (ages 10 to 12).

Obviously there's a big difference between a newborn and a three-year-old (try carrying a three-year-old in a car carrier if you don't believe me). There's also a striking difference between your kindergartener, who loves school and loves her teacher and loves all the kids in her class, and your sixth grader, who only likes recess and thinks his teacher is too strict and is sure the other kids in the class think he's a nerd. On the other hand, your seventh grader may be into makeup and pop music, while your best friend's seventh grader is still playing with Legos and watching Marc Brown's "Arthur" on PBS after school.

In other words, there's no pigeonholing kids—or adults, for that matter. But there are some general characteristics we can expect to see as our children grow and change. I suspect you'll recognize your own children somewhere along the continuum.

INFANT & TODDLER (UP TO AGE 3) • • • • • • • • • • • • • •

Physical growth and change is at its most stunning at the beginning of life. The tiny fingers babies are born with are big enough to throw a ball and hold a spoon by the time they're three. Somewhere around twelve months, most children start walking, and right around the same time, they begin using words for familiar people and objects.

Children this age learn through their senses—especially taste, as you may have noticed when your two-year-old tried to eat the pen you left on the coffee table. Rather than playing *with* other children, they're mainly playing *alongside* other children. As they try to figure out the boundaries between themselves and others, they may seem contrary and negative at times. It's important to remember that behavior that appears stubborn or contrary to us as adults is simply a toddler's way of exploring her role in her family and her world.

A child's understanding of God at this age generally consists of an extra-special, big person who made everything. This is the perfect time of life to begin learning the concept of a loving, creator God who always cares, just as Mommy and Daddy care. As we rock, cuddle and comfort our young children, we not only contribute to their early understanding of God's love but also build a concept of security and trust in the One who loves us most.

PRESCHOOL (AGES 3-5) ••••••••••••••••••••••

At this age, large muscles are developing, so running, hopping, and jumping are important growth activities. Small motor skills may lag behind, but they're typically improving enough that children can dress themselves and begin drawing recognizable pictures.

Preschoolers have many questions about the world around them as they try to figure out how things work—thus the incessant "why's." They know, down to the last detail, exactly in what order their day is supposed to go (first the clothes and then the breakfast—never, ever, the other way around) but are often confused by time concepts, such as *yesterday* and *tomorrow*. If the big trip to the zoo isn't happening until next week, for example, don't mention it until the night before or you'll be answering "When are we going to the zoo?" until you're blue in the face.

Relationships with others are becoming more and more important at this age, so it is a good time to emphasize biblical concepts such as helping one another. Many churches begin Christian education at age three. Preschool children enjoy learning simple Bible stories that teach about God's love for all people.

ELEMENTARY (AGES 5-10) •

Children are still growing rapidly at this age, and somewhere in this stage their coordination will improve enough that they can play an instrument or try a sport. They learn to read, start to have empathy for others, and begin to form opinions of their own. What an exciting time of life!

Grade schoolers have an increasing interest in social groups, and they begin to pay attention to the differences between boys and girls. They're learning to work together in groups, though they may prefer doing things on their own. And they're wavering between wanting to be grown-up and wishing to remain Mommy and Daddy's little boy or girl. Even as they begin to explore the world on their own terms, they desperately need the strong, supportive presence of their parents.

At this age, children can use the Bible to look up familiar passages. With encouragement, they can recognize how Jesus' teachings fit their own lives. They can learn to pray by themselves when they want to talk to God. They're beginning to make their faith their own, and they need their parents to model living and active faith.

PRETEEN (AGES 10-12) •••••••••••••••••••••••

How often have you heard (or said), "I wouldn't be that age again for any amount of money?" Certainly pre-adolescence can be a painful time of life, with the quick rate of physical development and the sudden infusion of hormones that tends to leave kids wondering where on earth they fit in. Their rapid mood swings may make you wonder as well.

As they approach the teenage years, children gain the ability to grasp abstract ideas and tackle philosophical dilemmas. It's a great time for us parents to take advantage of these skills to engage our kids in important conversations. Recent brain research, however, indicates that capacity for logical thought decreases dramatically at this age. Keep that in mind when your twelve-year-old daughter opens a package of cereal upside down and watches its contents scatter all over the kitchen floor. Honestly, she can't help it. Count to ten, keep your cool, and remind yourself of her good qualities. Repeat.

This is an important time to remember how different all kids are, and to respect those differences. Don't be swayed by the horror stories you hear from other parents—remember that no two kids are alike and that yours are especially precious. No matter how different your preteen son appears from the darling, cuddly baby you rocked so many years ago, he's still the same person and still needs your love and attention.

At this age, kids are able to cement the personal relationship with God they've been building all their lives. They can understand Jesus as a real person who walks alongside them in good and bad times. They're capable of applying their faith, rather than just learning about it.

Making Faith Fun

As you use this book, keep these general characteristics in mind. They can help you make the most of your child's developmental capabilities.

Now, take a look at the chapters and select one that describes situations you'd like to connect with a living, active faith. Give some of the suggested activities a try and see what happens. And may the Lord be with you!

CHAPTER TWO

On the Road

Going to church no more makes you a Christian
than sleeping in your garage makes you a car.
—*Garrison Keillor*

Whether you're dashing from errand to errand after a long day at work or you're in the family van for a cross-country trip, hauling the kids around can be a challenge. Bruce and I have resorted to the "don't make me pull this van over" threat more often than we care to remember. In fact, on a recent trip home from church, the commotion behind us was so out of control that Bruce did, indeed, pull onto a side street to avoid swerving into oncoming traffic. By silent agreement, he and I simply sat there for a full five minutes before the kids quieted down enough to notice that we weren't moving. Unfortunately, we were both so fed up with the behavior of our offspring that we didn't think quickly enough to turn the situation into a faith-filled learning experience. Somehow, confinement in a vehicle with three fussy children didn't bring out the best in us.

But on another day, when the Holy Spirit granted us an extra measure of parental patience, we stumbled into a game we named "What If?" Bruce and I had been talking with some other parents at church about helping our kids call on God to resist peer pressure. So I tossed out a hypothetical situation: "What if all the other kids at a sleepover wanted to watch a video you know we wouldn't approve of?"

In no time at all, Kayla was sharing a time when that exact thing had happened to her. Then Layney and Garrett came up with ideas to try if it ever happened to them.

We discovered that time in the van can be the perfect time to connect with each other and with our faith—if we managed to think of it before the back seat turned into a three-ring circus. After all, when you're on the road you've got a captive audience (though at times you may feel like you're the one being held captive). Try some of these age-appropriate suggestions for making the most of your driving time.

FOR ALL AGES ····························

Pick Your Music

Putting on some music can help keep the back-seat passengers from becoming too restless. Have some recordings of faith-based music available. Try something by a favorite Christian performer. Leave the same tape or CD in your vehicle for several weeks at a time. If you listen to the same songs over and over, your kids will be able to sing along. At the same time, they'll be learning scriptural messages they can carry with them wherever they go.

INFANT & TODDLER (UP TO AGE 3) . . . .

Sing, Sing, Sing

And sing some more. Bruce and I remember singing to our babies until we were hoarse. It was the only way to keep away the "I'm-sick-of-this-car-seat" fussies. The sound of your voice, even if you can't carry a tune in a bucket, is much more enthralling to kids this age than the voice of a stranger on a recording. If your toddler starts to fuss, change to a silly voice to get her attention. Build a repertoire of favorite Bible songs. (You'll find suggestions at the end of this chapter.)

Notice God's Creation

Play a simple game of spotting as many things as you can that were created by God. You'll find people, animals, trees, clouds and flowers. Even if your three-year-old calls out, "Telephone pole," relate the pole to the huge tree God made that people turned into a pole for our telephone lines. It's a safe bet you won't see a single thing that can't be traced back, somewhere in its history, to something God created.

Peek-a-Boo!

Peek-a-boo is an excellent developmental game for infants and toddlers. It appeals to their sense of anticipation and to their need to be assured that loved ones who disappear will come back. Try it next time someone else is driving. With your little one in a car seat in the back, play peek-a-boo from your front seat—with one little twist that will plant a seed of faith. Hide below the head rest, and then pop saying, "Peek-a-boo, God loves you!" Try it again with "Peek-a-bee, God loves me!" This simple game will keep very young children happy for a surprisingly long time.

PRESCHOOL (AGES 3-5) ·

Keep Singing

When children are still in car seats, they need a lot of interaction to keep them from remembering they're strapped down. They'll probably enjoy recordings of Bible songs at this age. Enhance your drive time by playing songs that will help your kids remember the Bible stories they're learning in Sunday School.

Tell a Story

Tell a favorite Bible story. Tell it again and again. You'll get tired of the story long before your child does—kids this age thrive on repetition. After the first two or three hundred retellings, my husband started changing details and waited for our daughter to correct him. Sometimes I paused at crucial points and let her fill in the blanks. Before long, she was able to tell the whole story herself without help. Internalizing scripture stories in the early years lays the cornerstone for a strong foundation of faith.

Everywhere a Sign, Part I

Look for traffic signs and help your preschooler learn what each means. Kids this age are becoming very aware of rules—and what happens when they're broken. Talk about how signs are like rules that keep us safe, and relate that concept back to the rules God gives us to keep us safe and help us live together peacefully. The language of the Ten Commandments will be beyond preschoolers' understanding, but they can certainly relate to God's wish for us to love one another, to share with others, and to be kind to everyone we meet.

Point Out Helpers

As you drive, ask your kids to look for construction workers, emergency service people, or bank tellers—anyone who's doing a job that helps others or the community. Remind them how blessed your family is that God creates so many different people with so many different gifts. Say a quick thank-you to God for all those people who are helping.

Keep Your Eye on the Cross

Have your kids be on the lookout for items that remind them of the cross. Suggest that the telephone poles, the letter "t" on a sign—whatever they might find—can remind them of Jesus in our world.

"I'm Thinking of Someone..."

In this variation on "I Spy," give your preschooler clues to guess familiar Bible story characters. For example, "I'm thinking of someone whose name started with 'N,' who listened to God and built a great big boat." After you've played a few times, your child's likely to want to think of a character for you to guess. And we found that by coming up with silly answers to our kids' clues (for example, "someone whose name starts with 'B' and had his eyes healed by Jesus"..."Big Bird? Barney?"), we could keep the game going a lot longer.

ELEMENTARY (AGES 5-10) ....

Sing Some More

Your grade schooler's tastes in music are probably changing, but you may still be dealing with sibling squabbles in the back seat. Stick with music that has a message of faith, but challenge kids to come up with their own Bible-based lyrics. Bruce and I have been reduced to tears of laughter listening to our kids' silly words about Noah, for example with "The Arky Arky Song," they came up with: "God said to Noah, the ark's gonna get all yucky, yucky, Watch out for those animals, and don't step in their mucky, mucky...." What a great way for the family to learn that faith is fun!

Pray for a Stranger

Children this age are learning to have empathy for others. Any time a police car, fire truck, or ambulance races past with sirens and lights, point out that it means someone is ill, hurt, or in danger. Say a simple prayer asking God to watch over, protect, and help the emergency personnel and whoever needs their assistance.

Bible ABC's

In this game, driver and passengers can take turns naming something or someone from the Bible that begins with each letter of the alphabet: A is for Abraham, B is for Bartholomew, C is for Canaan, etc. (You can look forward to consulting a Bible concordance together to find words for "Q" or "X"—we discovered Queen of Sheba and Xerxes).

Make a List

A variation on the "Bible ABC's" game is to list as many Bible characters, events or places as you can for each letter of the alphabet. When you run out of ideas for "A," move on to "B." To make this game more challenging, change the parameters for your lists. Try listing women from the Old Testament, for example, or miraculous events. On a long trip, take a children's Bible along so they can look up additional items for the lists.

"What If?"

Car time is a great time to bring up challenging scenarios and take turns figuring out how to handle them. Often the lack of face-to-face contact in the car will help kids open up. Here are some suggestions: "What if a friend offered you a cigarette?" "What if no one would sit at the same lunch table with the unpopular girl at school?" "What if all the other girls at a sleepover wanted to watch a movie you know we wouldn't approve of?" They'll probably start thinking up their own questions, and you can try answering them too.

Bruce and I were thrilled when this game brought up some situations our kids had actually faced. Kayla related a time when she had felt pressured at a slumber party, and Layney suggested she could have gotten all the girls involved in a game, instead. Layney told of her discomfort at the way some of the girls in her class treat each other, and Garrett told her what he had said one time when he'd been in the same boat. We parents listened, jumping in occasionally with questions about what God would have wanted, and were thrilled to hear them sharing!

PRETEEN (AGES 10-12) ·····················

More Music

If your preteen is interested in contemporary Christian music, keep it on hand. If not, go ahead and listen to a popular radio station. Uncomfortable with the messages you hear in the lyrics? What about the clothing (or lack thereof) worn by some of the artists? Is the on-air chatter questionable—or downright inappropriate? Don't shut off the radio in disgust. Ask preteens open-ended questions and listen to their opinions. Here are some suggestions: "What do you think this person is trying to say about _____?" "How does that match with what you believe to be true?" "What have we learned from the Bible that supports this?" "What would happen if everyone who listened to this song decided to behave in a way that reflected these ideas?" Keep in mind, too, that many secular songs in the pop genre do have spiritual depth. You may be surprised how thought-provoking modern music can be.

Everywhere a Sign, Part II

Billboards can be a catalyst for a faith-based conversation with your preteen. In larger cities, you'll find advertisements for anything from radio stations' racy publicity stunts to triple-X-rated theaters. We've run across equally disturbing billboards in more rural areas, such as signs for establishments labeled "Gentlemen's Clubs"—surely an oxymoron. Unlike radio stations, which we can turn off if we don't care for them, all passersby are subjected to questionable messages on billboards. Your preteen is old enough to engage in a discussion about the effects of such advertisements on young children, and on older kids who don't have a caring adult in their lives to help them process these images. Recall Jesus' words in Matthew: "If any of you put a stumbling block before one of these little ones who believe in me, it would be better for you if a great millstone were fastened around your neck and you were drowned in the depth of the sea" (18:6). Consider with your child the balance between Jesus' concern for the children and our constitutional rights to freedom of speech and press.

Point/Counterpoint

Use the increasing polarization of religious and political groups in our nation to challenge preteens to defend their beliefs. You may find this a challenge as well. As you drive, bring up a controversial issue from the daily news or something you hear on the radio. Take a stand, pro or con, and challenge them to argue the opposite side.

Bruce and I found we were forced to reach deep for why we believe what we believe. Explain how your faith in God helps you decide where you stand on the issue. You'll be making a lasting statement about the connection between faith and everyday life. You will also help your child gain empathy and understanding for people with viewpoints opposite of yours. A word of caution, however. This kind of debate can bring up some strong emotions. Be careful to listen to what your child has to say, and step lightly.

It may not be easy to keep your faith topmost in your mind as you drive. The distractions of traffic, back-seat bickering, and errands all get in the way. You might need to wait to try out these activities until you have another adult with you—one to focus on safe driving, the other on living faith opportunities. Just keep trying, keep sharing your faith, and keep listening. And by the time you're back in your garage, you may already see the benefits of turning your drive time into a time of active faith.

SIMPLE BIBLE SONGS . . . .

"Jesus Loves and Cares for Me"
(to the tune of "Mary Had a Little Lamb")
Jesus loves and cares for me,
Cares for me,
Cares for me,
Jesus loves and cares for me,
Every single day.

"Let the Children Come to Me"
(also to "Mary Had a Little Lamb")
Let the children come to me,
Come to me,
Come to me,
Let the children come to me,
That's what Jesus said.

"Noah's Boat"

(to the tune of "London Bridge")
Noah built a great big boat
Great big boat,
Great big boat,
Noah built a great big boat,
Then the rain came down.
An-i-mals all went inside,
Went inside,
Went inside,
An-i-mals all went inside,
When the rain came down.
God put a rainbow in the sky,
In the sky,
In the sky,
God put a rainbow in the sky,
To show God's covenant.

"Love Your Neighbor"

(to the tune of "Frère Jacques")
Love your neighbor,
Love your neighbor,
Jesus said,
Jesus said.
Who's my neighbor?
Who's my neighbor?
Eve-ry-one.
Eve-ry-one.

"David and the Giant"

(to the tune of "Ten Little Indians")
David fought a great big giant,
David fought a great big giant,
David fought a great big giant
Because he trusted God.
Daniel went in with the lions,
Daniel went in with the lions,
Daniel went in with the lions,
Because he trusted God.
I can do whatever God asks,
I can do whatever God asks,
I can do whatever God asks,
Because I trust in God.

"B-I-B-L-E"

(to the tune of "B-I-N-G-O")
There is a book God gave to me,
I read it every day.
B-I-B-L-E, B-I-B-L-E, B-I-B-L-E
And it shows me the way.

"I'm a Child of God!

(to the tune of "If You're Happy and You Know It")
Oh, I'm a child of God, yes I am!
Oh, I'm a child of God, yes I am!
From my eyes and my nose,
To my knees and my toes,
Oh, I'm a child of God, yes I am!

"Animals in the Ark"

(to the tune of "Old MacDonald")
The duckies [chickens, piggies, etc.] went in-to the ark,
To get out of the rain.
And on this ark they had a roof,
To get out of the rain.
With a quack, quack here,
And a quack, quack there,
Here a quack, there a quack,
Everywhere a quack, quack,
The duckies went into the ark
To get out of the rain.

CHAPTER THREE

AT THE STORE

Preach the Gospel at all times.
When necessary use words.
—St. Francis of Assisi

The phrase "shop till you drop" takes on a whole new meaning when the kids are along. Between their begging to push the cart, disappearing as they hide under the clothes racks, and insisting they must have the newest artificially-flavored toaster pastry, I often want to drop before I even enter the store.

I wish I could say it gets easier as they get older, but that hasn't been our experience. Just last week, we went to buy paint supplies at a home improvement store (some form of temporary insanity made us think dragging the kids along on this expedition was a good idea). Between bickering over which sibling should be allowed to play the "drums" on the paint cans and the oh-so-innocent kick at the sister's face as one child tried to climb into the cart, Bruce and I both felt we deserved medals when all three kids made it out of the store alive. No, children's behavior doesn't necessarily improve as they age. But through trial and error, through many jaw-breaking, clenched-teeth moments, we have managed to collect a bag of tricks that can keep us from totally losing our cool. Praying for patience is the number one trick. When we keep praying, keep learning, and keep on practicing activities like those in this chapter, even a shopping trip can turn into an experience of living faith.

INFANT & TODDLER (UP TO AGE 3) . . . .

feed the Hungry, Part I

Create a permanent category on your shopping list titled "Items for the Needy." Any time you're at the store, pick up a few cans of food or a tube of toothpaste to be taken to your church donation box or a local relief agency. As you choose these items, talk with your children in a very matter-of-fact way about our calling to care for those in need: "Some people don't have enough money to buy food. I think God wants us to pick out some good things to give them." The earlier we teach our children the value of helping others, the more natural their response will become.

"I Can Help!"

Once children learn to walk, keeping them in a stroller or shopping cart safety seat becomes a struggle. Sometimes it helps to give in and let them walk. If you keep them occupied with simple, helpful tasks, they'll be less likely to run off and leave you in the dust. Let your kids carry the shopping list, lift small items off a low shelf for you, or set nonbreakables in the cart. Praise them for their help, explaining that when we work together and help each other, we're doing what God wants us to do. Keep them busy enough, and before long they'll wear out and ask to sit in the cart again!

Keep Praying

At this age, shopping with children can be a matter of survival. I can remember being so busy trying to keep a squirmy infant or toddler safely in her seat that I could hardly keep a corner of my mind on what it was I went to the store to get. How can an exasperated parent keep it together? Remember that God wants us to pray about everything, even a simple shopping trip. Ask the Holy Spirit to guide you and keep you calm and sane as you try to keep your little one's surprisingly long arms from grabbing a pickle jar and sending it crashing to the floor. There have been times when I've lost my temper and reacted to my children in ways that were most un-Christ-like. On those occasions when we lose it, we can tell God we're sorry, tell our children we're sorry—and keep praying.

You might even try turning to your child and saying, "We're both having a hard time today. I'm going to ask God to help us." And then pray something short and sweet, such as, "God, help me to be kind, and help [your child's name] to be calm." Your child might not understand exactly what you are saying, but the message will come through that it's good to ask God for help.

PRESCHOOL (AGES 3-5) •••••••••••••••••••••

Feed the Hungry, Part II

Continue a family tradition of regularly purchasing food and toiletries for those who need them. Now that your children's likes and dislikes are becoming increasingly pronounced, ask them to help choose what to buy, even if their choices seem unorthodox. The first time our youngest picked out bubblegum-flavored toothpaste and a bag of marshmallows, I overruled his choices and he was crushed. Later I thought it over and wished I'd let him have his way. After all, I finally realized, if I were getting groceries for my family at a food pantry, wouldn't I like to find something fun and unusual to take home? And didn't I run the risk of squelching our son's generous impulses when I struck down his ideas? On our next trip to the store, I let him have free reign in his food-pantry choices. Then I added a few cans of green beans to our offering to include a healthier choice.

"It's for You!"

As much as children this age want things for themselves, they also take great pride in giving to others. Take advantage of this generosity to create a distraction when you start hearing the "gimme's." Make a show of picking out something special for another family member. Here's what worked for Bruce one particularly trying day: "You know, your sister's been having a hard time at school this week. Let's buy the ingredients to make her favorite supper to cheer her up. What does she like best? What do we need to buy to make it?" He provided a great example of how to put others before ourselves, as Jesus taught.

Lend a Hand

When you see someone at the store struggling with packages or with a door, jump in to help. Have your preschooler help you hold the door open or pick up a dropped bag. Point out to her the way she followed Jesus' commandment to love one another and to "do to others as you would have them do to you" (Matthew 7:12).

feed the Hungry, Part III

Continue to allow your children to help choose items to donate to your local food collection center. Encourage them to use their knowledge of healthy eating habits to pick out everything needed to create one complete, nutritious meal for a family in need.

Needs vs. Wants

Use your shopping time to spark a discussion of the difference between what we truly need to grow and be healthy and what we merely want for more selfish reasons. Remind your kids that Jesus told us not to worry about what we eat, drink or wear. Jesus also taught us to "be on your guard against all kinds of greed; for one's life does not consist in the abundance of possessions" (Luke 12:15). (But don't be afraid to give in on a purely "want" item every now and then. We all deserve a treat on a special occasion!)

Turn the Other Cheek

At some point, we've all run into cashiers, shelf stockers, and managers who give us the opposite of "service with a smile." We can take a deep breath, say a quick prayer, and use our imaginations to consider what might be happening in this person's life that would cause him or her to be so unpleasant. We can respond with kindness, remembering that Jesus asks us to "bless those who curse you, pray for those who abuse you" (Luke 6:28). Elementary-aged kids are likely to pick up on this subtle witness.

But our failings can provide a good lesson, as well. Recently, when I got an earful from a tired and overworked cashier, I answered back with an unpleasant retort. Our daughter asked me about it afterward, and we talked about my inability to turn the other cheek. I think she appreciated knowing that even grown-ups can have trouble living the way God wants us to live.

Keep the Change

Any time you pay in cash, collect the change and put it in a special container. As a family, choose a service organization to donate the money to at the end of a given time period. Each time you put change in the container, talk with your kids about how that money will be used. Then leave the container out in a prominent place as a visual reminder.

Paper or Plastic?

We hear this question so often, why not turn the answer into an act of faith? Keeping in mind our responsibility to be good stewards of the earth, make a decision as a family about how you'll take your purchases home each time. If you choose paper, make a plan to recycle the bags to conserve trees. If you choose plastic, find ways to reuse the bags, or find a plastic bag recycling bin (we have one in our grocery store). Another option would be to purchase or make reusable tote bags to take with you each time you shop. Take the time to explain to your kids what you're doing—and why. Get them involved. Take them with you to the recycling center or enlist their help in making tote bags. Ask them for suggestions about what else you might recycle.

Daily Bread

If your grocery store is like ours, there's a staggering array of choices when you're buying bread. One entire forty-foot long, four-shelf high aisle is packed with bread, buns, rolls and English muffins. Talk with your children about this abundance and compare it with the petition in the Lord's Prayer, "Give us this day our daily bread" (Matthew 6:11). Ask them to consider if all that bread on the shelves will get bought and eaten before it goes bad. Ask what your family might do to help others receive their daily bread. Get your kids thinking about what it might be like to get by without so many choices. (Mention that the Israelites made it through the desert for forty years with only manna.) Ask them what they think about the vast selection in our stores.

Feed the Hungry, Part IV

Give your son three or four dollars to buy enough food to make supper for the entire family. He'll see quickly that it's nearly impossible to stretch his dollars far enough, and he'll understand much more vividly why people earning minimum wage must often depend on emergency relief agencies. Give him a few hints about cheap foods to look for (store-brand tuna, rice, beans, etc.) and help him follow through as he prepares the meal. At the end of your meal, pray for those who struggle to feed their families, and renew your family's commitment to contributing to the local food pantry.

Three Measures of Flour

If your child enjoys working in the kitchen, challenge her to come up with a meal that consists only of foods mentioned in the Bible. Suggestions might be flour, lamb, fish, milk, honey, eggs, figs, salt, spices and yeast. I'm not a particularly adventurous cook, but my husband enjoyed tackling this meal with our daughter. You may end up with an unusual menu, and it will be an opportunity to discuss the foods God has always provided.

From Here to There

On a day when errands have piled up so high you're afraid the mountain might come tumbling down, ask your older child to plan out a shopping route for you. Request that she try to cut as many miles as possible off the trips from one stop to another to conserve fuel and reduce pollution. Have her see if any of the errands could be done via the internet to avoid more traveling, again remembering our responsibility to care for God's creation.

"Do not worry about...what you will wear" (Luke 12:22)

When your son has grown out of all his clothes yet again, take him to a thrift shop that benefits a local service organization. He may find unique or retro clothes that appeal to him, and you'll be both saving money and helping the service organization. Even if he doesn't find anything he's willing to wear, he can gain an appreciation of what it might be like for kids his age whose families can't afford to shop in pricier stores. Make a point of praying with him, thanking God for giving your family the resources that allow you to make choices.

At this age your kids will be dealing with pressure to purchase the latest hot name brands of clothing and shoes worn by their peers. Even if these items are within your price range, you might want to make a connection between desire for these popular brands and the tenth commandment, warning us against coveting our neighbors' belongings.

The Golden Idol

Be on the lookout for opportunities to discuss with your preteen the runaway consumerism in our culture. As you shop, pay attention to ads and packaging that feed into our need to feel popular, important or beautiful. Compare this to the worship of Baal and other idols that so disappointed God. Our idols today may not come in the shape of a golden calf, but they are idols just the same. Talk about what we can do to resist pressure to grab and buy, and instead focus on our relationship with God.

Bruce brought this point home to our whole family one long, rainy Saturday. We had been stepping over each other all day long. Our house, which is quite small compared to the homes of many of our friends, seemed to be shrinking by the minute. Exasperated, I let out a wail of despair over the lack of space, my need for a private office, and our general misfortune. Calmly and with a trace of amusement in his voice, my husband suggested we try living in a hut in Africa for a while instead. Though I didn't want to admit it, I knew he had a healthier perspective than I did. Thanks to God's grace, I managed to laugh at myself, and we all offered a prayer of thanksgiving for God's gifts.

The next time you go shopping with your children, help them be aware of how incredibly blessed they are. When your kids—or you—find yourself longing for the latest gadget or the coolest clothes, recall Jesus' words in Luke: "And do not keep striving for what you are to eat and what you are to drink, and do not keep worrying… your Father knows that you need them. Instead, strive for his kingdom, and these things will be given to you as well" (12:29-31).

In your prayers with your kids, name those near and far who go without sufficient food, clothing and shelter every day. Humbly thank God for providing you and your family with what you need. Cultivating this thankful attitude on a daily basis will make faith come alive in your family.

CHAPTER FOUR

CHORE TIME

Anything big enough to occupy our mind
is big enough to hang a prayer on.
—*George MacDonald*

I've often been guilty of praying only for the big things: help in finding a job, health for a sick relative, peace in war-torn areas. I also know that we're taught in Philippians 4:6: "Do not worry about anything, but in everything by prayer and supplication with thanksgiving let your requests be made known to God." Over time, I've come to appreciate the word "everything" in that lesson. I'm finding that if I remember to pray about everything—even mundane, frustrating things like trying to get the kids to do their daily chores—I do experience the "peace of God" that's promised in the very next verse (Philippians 4:7).

But getting the kids to do their chores can be hard enough without trying to turn it into a faith-building exercise. Housework is a fact of life, especially if you're as adverse as Bruce and I are to living with toys and dirty clothes piled up to our eyeballs. We've tried to get our kids involved in the daily upkeep of the house ever since they were old enough to flick a dust rag over the coffee table. But too often we've ended up shouting, threatening, and generally falling short of Christ's model of loving patience.

So, we figured, what did we have to lose by trying to turn chore time into something thought-provoking, even something fun? Give these tips a try, and see how they help you live your faith—and maybe even retain your sanity!

INFANT & TODDLER (UP TO AGE 3) . . . .

Diaper Changing

Even when you've changed so many diapers you have to check twice to make sure you got the last one on the right end, try not to let it get you down. Use those few minutes of one-on-one time to connect with your little one. Tweak a tummy, a leg, and a finger, chanting along:

> God made baby's tummy,
> God made baby's knee,
> God made baby's fingers,
> And God made me!"

Both of you will be reminded of God's power of creation, and the baby's giggles might help you forget that this is the twentieth diaper you've changed today.

Washed Clean, Part I

Supper's over, the dishes need washing, and your son is so caked with food you don't dare let him out of his high chair yet. Bruce came up with an entertaining solution to this after-supper challenge: Give your toddler a wet wash cloth and let him wipe his own tray and face. It wasn't until all three of our kids were out of high chairs that I overheard another dad use the same activity as an opportunity to talk about how Jesus makes us all clean by forgiving us for the messes we make. What a simple and lovely reminder!

Time to Get Dressed

With very young children, getting dressed can be a frustrating and time-consuming chore. First, you have to convince your child daily that taking off pajamas and putting on clothes is non-negotiable. Then there's the haggle over which clothing is appropriate for the weather. Finally comes the wrestling match to get the clothes on as your kid tries to run (or crawl) off to play. You may feel your store of parental patience is bankrupt before the day has a chance to get started.

The most important lesson Bruce and I learned about this scenario was to simply let it go. If there's nowhere you've got to get to any time soon, let your toddler run off half naked. Just say to yourself Jesus' words in Matthew 6:28: "And why do you worry about clothing?" If you're on your way out the door and your little one is wearing the striped blue shirt with the purple polka-dot pants, mittens on her feet, and socks on her hands, remember that Jesus continually associated with the outcasts of society. If he could love people who looked "weird," you can too!

PRESCHOOL (AGES 3-5) ••••••••••••••••••••

Mary and Martha

Tidying up a room can be an overwhelming task for preschoolers, especially if there are several kinds of toys out at once. Kids at this age love pretend play, so give a quick recap of the conflict between the sisters Mary and Martha (Luke 10:38-42). Then take turns with your child being Mary or Martha, while both of you sing to the tune of "Here We Go Round the Mulberry Bush":

> This is how Martha picks up the blocks,
> [or cars, or dolls, or whatever toys are out]
> Picks up the blocks, picks up the blocks.
> This is how Martha picks up the blocks,
> While Mary sits and listens.

When the room's all tidy, reward yourselves by reading together (and listening to, like Mary) a Bible story.

Productive Graffiti

When there are many tasks to be done, or one task that lasts longer than a preschoolers' limited attention span, your kids need a built-in break. Tape a big sheet of paper to a wall and set out a box of washable crayons or markers. As you work together on the chores, retell some of their favorite Bible stories. When they need a breather, have them work on a mural of scenes from the stories, while you continue with the chores. Once they're ready to move on from the graffiti-making, give them another simple chore to accomplish.

Number Pick-Up

Another way to keep preschoolers focused on the toy pick-up is to break it up into manageable segments. Ask questions such as the following and pick up the number of toys that matches the answers:

Q: "How many of each animal went on the ark?"
A: "Two!"
Pick up two toys.
Q: "How many loaves of bread did Jesus have to feed all the people?"
A: "Five!"
Pick up five toys.
Q: "How many disciples did Jesus have?"
A: "Twelve!"
Pick up twelve toys.

It won't matter that your child won't know the answers to many of the questions. It won't even matter if you don't know some of the answers yourself. You can guess together and check in a Bible later. Following up by reading the Scripture verse will make a big impression.

Washed Clean, Part II

When the table, countertop or window becomes grubby with food and fingerprints, let your preschooler help scrub it clean. Compare the old, dirty surface with how we feel when we've done something wrong. Compare the new, clean surface with how we feel when we remember that Jesus made us clean, washing away all those things we've done wrong.

ELEMENTARY (AGES 5-10) ....

Pass the Baton, Part I

Making out the grocery list can become a burden week after week. Let your school-age children give you a hand with this one. Dictate a list to them while you're taking care of another chore, such as doing the dishes or starting supper. Take it a step further and allow them to make some choices about what goes on the list. If your kids are anything like our son, the choices might gravitate toward sugar-coated or fat-laden items. Discuss the wisdom of some of those choices, pointing out that God created us with the ability to make decisions. Sometimes we want to do only what seems like fun at the time, but God sends the Holy Spirit to help guide our decisions. Our son inevitably ends up picking out a box of Chocolaty Frosted Sugar Bombs, but Bruce and I know we've at least planted a seed.

Stage a Chore Strike, Part I

Look for a time when the griping about chores seems especially loud (we don't have to wait long at our house). Allow one family member at a time to quit doing all her chores for a few days. The table may get so sticky you can't get the plates off it after supper, but hang in there. As disorder and chaos begin to take over, point out how this experiment illustrates Paul's words in 1 Corinthians 12:21: "The eye cannot say to the hand, 'I have no need of you,' nor again the head to the feet, 'I have no need of you.'" Thank each other for what each one does to keep the family—your body of believers—going. And thank God for giving each of you the ability to do the jobs that need to be done.

"It's a Tough Job"

Intentionally assign your child a task that's too hard for him. Watch carefully and be ready to step in to help before he's had time to get frustrated. Point out how the Holy Spirit steps in to give us help, sometimes when we don't even ask, because God always knows exactly what we need, as we're promised in Romans 8:26: "The Spirit helps us in our weakness...but that very Spirit intercedes for us with sighs too deep for words."

Chore Swap

"He doesn't have nearly as many chores as I do. And all of his are easy ones!" Sound familiar? When your daughter insists that the grass is greener on her brother's side of the fence, suggest they swap chores for a few days. At the end of the agreed time, talk about how it felt to try and fill someone else's shoes. The siblings may choose to trade jobs permanently, or they may be desperate to return to their own chores. Either way, use the lesson as an opportunity to thank God for the different talents we're all given and for the many ways we're given to serve.

PRETEEN (AGES 10-12) •

Pass the Baton, Part II

Things were getting out of hand. Our youngest was wearing a dirty shirt for the third time in a week, and supper was going to be cold cereal if I forgot to stop at the store on the way home. Bruce hatched up the brilliant plan of letting our older daughter help us get organized. She had the computer skills to create a spreadsheet that would keep track of chores that needed to be remembered daily, weekly and monthly. Whether it's making a spreadsheet or a chart, or putting a schedule on the fridge, letting your child come up with a family plan is a great way to teach them that we each have different gifts (1 Corinthians 12:27-31).

Stage a Chore Strike, Part II

Complaints about household chores aren't likely to lessen with age. When the griping gets to you, go on strike yourself. Insist that your preteens do all their own laundry, cooking, shopping and cleaning for a few days. Things may be unbearably chaotic while you're on strike, or you may be pleasantly surprised by the way they step up to the plate. However things turn out, at the end of your strike you can talk together about what each of you needs to do to keep the family going and how living up to our responsibility is a way of showing love for each other. As you return to your chores, remind them of 1 John 4:19: "We love because [God] first loved us."

Look for Positives

Preteens tend to be especially sensitive to criticism. They're dealing with intense self-image issues ("Do I look okay?" "Do people like me?" "Am I normal?"). At an earlier stage, for example, we could ask our daughter to go back and dust the places she missed the first time, but as a preteen she takes such a request as a personal attack.

Bruce and I have to remind each other of this fact fairly often. We do try to choose our words carefully and be more aware of how we frame our requests so they don't sound like criticism. We also remind each other to "catch them being good." Though kids this age may try to hide it, compliments and approval from parents still mean a great deal to them. Give your child as much praise as you can, to counteract the negatives that are a part of being a preteen.

On nights when Bruce and I are facing each other across our bed, folding one last load of clothes at 10:30 P.M.—not out of any virtuous commitment to finishing our chores but rather so we can get the laundry off the bed and crawl under the covers before we fall asleep on our feet—it sometimes occurs to us that we're going to be doing this very same task for the rest of our lives. It's not the most cheerful thought to end the day with. But on a good day, the laundry, along with all the other never-ending tasks around the house, can remind us of the nature of faith building. It's a day-in, day-out job— one that's vital for the health and happiness of our family.

May the suggestions in this chapter help you make your faith a day-in, day-out part of your family's life.

CHAPTER FIVE

WHILE YOU WAIT

*A sure way to irritate people and to put evil thoughts
into their heads is to keep them waiting a long time.
This makes them immoral.*
—Friedrich Nietzsche

Seventh in line for the next available bank teller. An hour on the bleachers with our son during his sister's gymnastics class. The time warp of a doctor's waiting room crowded with sneezing, hacking toddlers. When I'm forced to wait, the thoughts in my head are more likely to be evil than loving or faith-filled. Throw a tired, whiny child into the mix and I'm one step away from saying or doing something unpleasant, if not downright immoral. And if it's that bad for me, I can only imagine how hard it is for the child, whose sense of time is about as accurate as a two-dollar watch.

We've learned that the number one survival tool in the waiting game is to make like a Boy Scout and be prepared. We plan for any given situation to take longer than we expect. It might help if we had Paul's words from Colossians 1:11 stamped on the backs of our hands: "May you be made strong with all the strength that comes from his glorious power, and may you be prepared to endure everything with patience."

Those times when we are able to "endure everything with patience," we have to give credit to that "strength that comes from his glorious power." We sure couldn't do it on our own. Through much trial and error, we've found a few tricks to help make our time spent waiting become an experience of faith.

INFANT & TODDLER (UP TO AGE 3) . . . .

Bag of Tricks

Within days of first-time parenthood, all parents learn the first rule of the diaper bag: Don't leave home without it. But as baby grows, the trusty diaper bag ends up being more than a mobile changing station; it becomes an entertainment center as well. It's a matter of survival to load the bag with bottles, snacks, pacifiers, anything that will keep your little one smiling. Why not include a Bible story book? Keep it lightweight (that bag's heavy enough as it is) and chewable (infants and toddlers prefer their books mouth-friendly).

Action Rhymes

Toddlers love action rhymes like "The Eensy, Weensy Spider." The rhyming is super for vocabulary development, and the hand movements give their motor skills a workout. You can help their faith grow as well by adding some faith-based action rhymes to your repertoire. Though the words may be too big a mouthful for them, children this age can mimic your actions. And the faith-based words you sing will plant a seed. (See the list at the end of this chapter for suggestions.)

Faith-Filled Snacks

When you have a toddler in tow, take-along snacks are a must. Keeping that little mouth busy and that tummy full can go a long way toward making your wait time bearable. The snacks you take with you can also be a reminder of your faith. Carry fish-shaped crackers and talk about times Jesus fed people with fish. Take pretzel sticks and make them into crosses before eating them. Put some O-shaped cereal in a baggy with pretzel sticks and use the sticks to "fish" out the cereal. Talk about Jesus' disciples catching fish with his help.

PRESCHOOL (AGES 3-5) ● ● ● ● ● ● ● ● ● ● ● ● ● ● ● ● ● ● ●

Action Rhymes Again

Preschoolers are pros when it comes to action rhymes. They perform the actions with energy and exuberance (make sure they have plenty of arm and leg room!). They're proud to be big enough to sing the words now, as well.

At this age they'll also begin to wonder about the meanings behind some of the words, so it's a good time to back up lyrics to biblical action rhymes (or any faith-based song) with an explanation of the story behind it. For example, the action rhyme "Jesus Feeds the People" found at the end of this chapter illustrates the feeding of the crowd in Matthew 15:29-39. You might read this story to your children from a Bible story book and discuss the many ways Jesus takes care of us.

Your Child's Bag of Tricks

At this age children probably don't require a diaper bag, but a travel bag of instant activities is a must for times when you're stuck waiting. Find a small backpack they can carry on their own. Sometime when you're not trying to get out the door for an appointment, spend some time helping them pack the bag with activities that can spark faith discussions. Bible storybooks are still a good waiting activity. Felt shapes are small and lightweight and can be used to create pictures anywhere you go. If you can find a non-breakable Noah's Ark set or nativity scene, put it in the backpack so you can take turns telling each other the story, using the people and animals as props.

The Old Drawing Board

If you don't normally carry a pad and pen in your purse, briefcase, or glove compartment, it's time to start. When our three were small, their scribbles could keep them occupied for a while, but soon Bruce or I would be pressed into service to draw whatever popped into their little heads. Neither of us ever advanced much beyond the stick person stage in our artistic abilities, but we could usually come up with something that satisfied them.

Ask your child to name a favorite Bible character or story, and draw something related. Or turn that idea around: Draw something from a Bible story you know your kids are familiar with, and see if they can guess what story you have in mind.

Body Part Inventory

This activity can work anywhere, but it's particularly appropriate while waiting in the doctor's examining room, when you're probably thinking about body parts anyway. Name different body parts and tell how they can remind you of God or of a Bible story. For example, eyes can make us think of blind Bartimeus and how Jesus helped him see again. Mouths can be used to sing a favorite Bible song. Hands can be folded to pray.

When Garrett suggested "toes," I was stumped at first. But he pointed out that Jesus and the disciples wore sandals, so their toes were probably pretty dirty most of the time. It doesn't matter how silly the conversation gets. The important point is that you're making an effort to keep Jesus in the front of your kids' minds, and you're making that wait time move just a little bit faster.

ELEMENTARY (AGES 5-10) ....

Noah's Ark Game

For a memory-stretcher, try this game: The first person starts out by saying, "God told Noah to build the ark and take the animals with him. First he took the camels."

The second person repeats that sentence, adding what Noah took second: "God told Noah to build the ark and take the animals with him. First he took the camels. Second he took the cows."

The next person repeats everything the second person said and adds what Noah took third, and so on. Keep playing until the list gets so long someone makes a mistake. End by saying together, "And God put a rainbow in the sky."

Memory Work

In many religious denominations, elementary-age children are asked to memorize items such as the Lord's Prayer, the Ten Commandments, and the Apostle's Creed. Memory work is, by some, considered outmoded. But committing words of faith to our memory and to our hearts can give us words of comfort to fall back on when we need them.

When you're stuck waiting in line, practice reciting the Lord's Prayer or the Ten Commandments. Truthfully, I had to look up the commandments when our kids were learning them for the first time. It surprised them to discover that Mama had some gaps in her religious training, but we had a good time learning together. The same was true of the names of the books of the Bible.

You might want to type up some prayers or comforting scripture verses that you want your kids to commit to memory. Keep a copy in your car. As you and your child sit and wait for a sibling's piano lesson to be finished, quiz each other on something you're trying to learn. Try reading a line and leaving out one or two words for your child to fill in. Change a word in a line or two and see if your child can correct you. Or take turns saying the piece you're trying to learn one word at a time, like this:

Dad: "Our"
Daughter: "Father"
Dad: "who"
Daughter: "art"
Dad: "in"
Daughter: "heaven"

This is trickier than it looks, but by the time you get to the end you'll know the words inside and out!

Memory Work Motions

While you're practicing that memory work, try making up motions to go along with the words. For example, start the Lord's Prayer by raising your arms to the sky as you say, "Our Father in heaven." For "Give us this day our daily bread," you might hold your hands out as if to receive the bread. Combining movement with the words helps kids to make the words their own.

"Where's the Coin?"

When we're stuck waiting, a coin game helps us pass the time. I can't imagine why guessing which hand a coin is in can keep our kids occupied, but it works. One time recently when we played this while waiting for our supper at a crowded restaurant, one of our kids asked why the words "In God we trust" were printed on one side of the coin. This question started an interesting discussion of religion and government, church and state, and Jesus' teachings about paying taxes (Matthew 22:15-22). Use other unexpected opportunities like this to share your beliefs and help your kids clarify what they believe.

Back to the Drawing Board

Keep that notepad and pen on hand for more sophisticated word games and drawing games with your preteen. Play games like the old stand-by, Hangman, but try to spell out the names of books of the Bible or biblical characters instead.

Actually, I've always felt uncomfortable with Hangman. When I was teaching elementary school, I changed the game to "spider" for a spelling review, with a spider hanging from a web. My students had to guess the word one letter at a time, and a leg got drawn on the spider for each incorrect guess. If the spider got all eight legs before the word was guessed, that round was over. To review Bible characters or books, you might draw a couple of "stone tablets" and mark incorrect guesses with Roman numerals, indicating the Ten Commandments.

Book Talk

It's the rule in our family that if there's any chance of wait time at a given event or appointment, we all need to have a book handy. Bruce and I have been amazed at the conversations that reading has sparked. We like to talk over with the kids what's going on in the books they read and to share with them what we're learning in our own books. Many times the discussions veer off in the direction of morals, ethics and values, and allow us to share with one another how our faith helps us interpret and apply what we read, in both fiction and non-fiction.

Show an interest in your child's reading, and you may be surprised by the way they (and you) stretch and grow!

Passing Notes

Note passing is an infamous pastime for preteens. Next time you're caught in a waiting situation with your preteen, try writing her a note. Quietly passing notes back and forth may appeal to her. Start off with something silly, maybe a lame "knock-knock" joke just to get her attention. Before you're out of time, though, write her a more meaningful message—maybe a prayer of thanksgiving for something special you see in her. In this way you can help her see how much you care for her, while also showing her an example of prayer in everyday life.

We are so accustomed to "instant" everything that waiting is becoming harder and harder. While visiting my mother-in-law recently, Bruce and I used her computer to check our home e-mail account. The thirty seconds we waited as her dial-up system tried to connect had me tapping my foot and huffing with impatience. Bruce paced the room in frustration. Realizing how ridiculously impatient we were being, we said a prayer of thanks for the gift of technology—as well as for the instant access we have in our own home.

The familiar passage from Ecclesiastes 3:1 reminds us that there is a time for everything. Sometimes the time that is given to us is simply a time to wait. I hope the activities in this chapter help you appreciate those times and use them as opportunities for your family to grow together.

FAITH-BASED ACTION RHYMES •••••••••••••••

"God Made Me!"

(to the tune of "I'm a Little Teapot")
God gave me fingers, [wiggle fingers]
God gave me hands, [wave hands]
God gave me legs so I can stand, [stand up]
God gave me two eyes so I can see, [blink eyes several times]
I'm so thankful God made me! [hug yourself]

"Jesus Hears Me When I Pray"

(to the tune of "Twinkle, Twinkle, Little Star")
I fold my hands so I can pray [fold hands]
In the night [lay head on hands as if sleeping]
or in the day, [pop head up and "wake up"]
When the sun shines oh, so bright, [raise arms in a circle over head]
When the stars are twinkling bright, [open and close hands like
        twinkling stars]
Jesus hears me when I pray [fold hands]
Every single word I say. [touch mouth]

"Counting Rhyme" (spoken)

One, two, [show first finger, then second]
God loves me and you. [point to self, others]
Three, four, [show third finger, then fourth]
Jesus knocks at our door. [knock on imaginary door]
Five, six, [show fifth finger, then sixth]
Jesus heals the sick. [hand to forehead, as if checking for a fever]
Seven, eight, [show seventh finger, then eighth]
Showing love is great. [hug each other]
Nine, ten, [show ninth finger, then tenth]
Jesus makes us clean again. [hold out one hand, palm up,
        and wipe it clean with the other hand]

"Jesus and the Children" (spoken)

This action rhyme works well if the adult starts and does every other line. Children can respond with "Yes, yes," and head nodding. It's a fun surprise when the response changes to "No, no," and head shaking.

Jesus was walking,
[make two fingers "walk" on palm of opposite hand]
Yes, yes. [nod head twice]
Jesus was talking, [open and close hand beside mouth]
Yes, yes. [nod head twice]
Mommies brought babies, [fold arms as if cradling a baby]
Yes, yes. [nod head twice]
Daddies brought children, [hold hands down low to indicate
            a small person]
Yes, yes. [nod head twice]
Disciples didn't like that, [fold arms and frown]
No, no. [shake head twice]
"Jesus is busy!" [shake finger as if scolding]
No, no! [shake head twice]
Jesus said, "Wait a minute!" [hold up a hand to indicate stop]
Yes, yes. [nod head twice]
"I love the children!" [hug yourself]
Yes, yes. [nod twice]
"Let the children come!" [wave "children" toward you]
Yes, yes! [nod twice]
"Let the children come!" [wave "children" toward you again]
Yes, yes! [nod twice)]

"Jesus feeds the People"

(to the tune of "Eensy, Weensy Spider")

Many, many people
came to see that day [point to many imaginary people in a crowd]
The son of God [make a cross with fingers]
To hear what he would say. [cup hand to ear]
They stood and watched [point to eyes]
And shuffled on their feet [shuffle feet]
Till all of them got hungry
and wanted food to eat. [rub tummy]
Jesus' twelve disciples
didn't have much food to share [hold out hands to show they're empty]
They didn't want to feed the crowd,
they didn't seem to care. [fold arms across chest and shake head]
Jesus took five loaves of bread [hold up five fingers]
And two little-bitty fish, [hold up two fingers]
And he made there be as much to eat
as anyone could wish.
[fold hands as if in prayer, then hold arms out wide as if in blessing]

CHAPTER SIX

THE GREAT OUTDOORS

The best remedy for those who are afraid, lonely or unhappy
is to go outside, somewhere where they can be quiet,
alone with the heavens, nature and God.
Because only then does one feel that all is as it should be
and that God wishes to see people happy,
amidst the simple beauty of nature.

—Anne Frank

Our family loves to take walks around the neighborhood, especially around twilight. Actually, there are usually three of us who want to go and two who protest. It's not always the same three and two split, but we rarely have one-hundred-percent agreement. But Bruce and I learned long ago that if we held out for unanimous decisions about anything to do as a family, we'd end up sitting in the living room and pouting twenty-four hours a day. So, whether everyone wants to or not, we all walk. And we ride our bikes. And we take trips to the park, and throw a ball around in the back yard, and go camping.

There's something about getting outside that brings us out of ourselves and our petty, daily worries. Maybe it's the smell of damp earth and freshly-cut grass or the feel of a fresh breeze on our faces. Maybe these sensory experiences are ways the Holy Spirit reminds us of God's presence.

I felt that presence particularly one evening when Layney, our second daughter, and I went out for a walk by ourselves. Everyone else was busy, and we enjoyed this "date" together. Both conversation and silence took on a special quality as we moved through the darkening neighborhood. At one point Layney confided in me that she hadn't liked taking walks when she was smaller. This came as no surprise. I remembered vividly the way she used to plop down on the sidewalk and refuse to move until we either got too far away for her comfort or Bruce and I gave in and carried her. What did surprise me, though, was the reason why she hadn't liked our walks. "I used to be afraid we'd get lost and never find our house again," she said

It was a perfect opening for me to tell my daughter about times when I'd been afraid of getting lost, in a larger sense. I talked about how, just as her father and I always watched over her and made sure she got home safely, God watches over us and helps us find our way.

I believe there was something about being out of doors that helped Layney confide in me and helped me share my beliefs and fears with her. I've noticed a similar openness when we've been camping, sitting around a fire with crickets and cicadas singing a chorus in the background. It's as if our usual barriers come down when we get away from home and possessions and get closer to God's creation.

Every day we hear on television and radio, in newspapers and magazines, that we need to get off the couch, get outside, and get moving. We know our bodies need the exercise. If getting outside and getting that exercise might also help us grow in faith as well, then what are we waiting for? Let's get going!

INFANT & TODDLER (UP TO AGE 3) . . . .

Blanket Time

Sometimes it's too much trouble to pack the diaper bag and force your toddler into the car seat, yet you're desperate to get out of the house. When these moments of cabin fever hit, some time in the back yard on a blanket might do the trick.

Take a few favorite toys and books outside and stretch out on the ground with your little one. Take a look at the grass and dirt surrounding the blanket. See if you can find any bugs to watch. Cast your eyes upward and notice the patterns made by the leaves and branches overhead as they move in the breeze. Make a point of talking to your toddler about our creative God who made all these things for us to enjoy. Even if your child's too young to understand your words, you'll be building a foundation of faith.

Go for a Stroll

The stroller can be a lifeline when you've been stuck in the house with a cranky infant all day. There were many times when Bruce and I, out of sheer desperation, loaded the kids up in our double stroller for a walk. Looking back, I can see the Holy Spirit's guidance at those times, telling us we needed to remove ourselves from the frustrations of housework and parenting for a while. Getting the family out in God's creation of trees, flowers, water and "wildlife"—even if it is only a squirrel and a few birds—can make it easier to let go of some of the littler things and see the bigger picture.

Experience Creation

While outside, collect leaves, sticks, rocks, and any other interesting artifacts you can find. Let your toddler feel each item (watching carefully to make sure things don't go in the mouth). Talk about how each piece feels to the touch, and emphasize how thankful we are that God made so many different textures—soft, rough, prickly, smooth, etc. Try sniffing each item. Give thanks for our sense of smell and the wide range of smells God created. Next see if you can make noises with anything you found. Snap a twig in two. Bang two rocks together. Thank God for giving us ears to hear these interesting sounds.

PRESCHOOL (AGES 3-5) ••••••••••••••••••••

Nature Cross

Help your preschooler gather sticks, blades of grass, and dandelion stems. Use them to make small crosses. See how many you can make, and compare them using important developmental vocabulary, such as "This cross is green," "This cross is big, but this one is small," or "This cross is bumpy, but this cross is smooth." Talk about the big cross Jesus was on, and what it might have been made of.

Bandage Cross

Self-adhesive bandages are a regular part of a preschooler's wardrobe. Bruce and I have always considered a bandage to be a mighty cheap placebo, and we dole them out freely.

When your child scrapes her knee jumping over a rock or coming down the slide too fast while playing outdoors, surprise her by putting on two bandages instead of one. Stick them on in the shape of the cross, and remind her that Jesus came to make all of our "owies" feel better.

Ark Animals

Although this game works indoors, you can really make the most of it outside. Name as many animals as you can think of and pretend to be those animals. Choose a place—maybe a big tree or an outdoor table—to be the "ark" and walk to it (remembering to stay in your animal character) to get out of the rain. Don't forget to imitate the noises your animal would make. Use the game to tell the story of Noah's Ark and how God took care of all the animals.

Cloud Watch

Flop down in the grass with your preschooler and spend some time watching the clouds overhead. Look for shapes that can remind your child of Bible stories: maybe Jonah's whale, Noah's ark, a cross, or the donkey that carried Mary to Bethlehem.

Look for Threes

To help your children consider the concept of the Holy Trinity, go on a search for outdoor items that come in threes. In our back yard there's plenty of clover, with three round leaves. Insects with their three distinct body parts are everywhere. Remember, though, that poison ivy has three leaves too! If you find any, it might elicit interesting questions from your preschooler. "What's poison ivy for?" or "Why did God make a plant that hurts us?" Don't panic if enlightening answers aren't on the tip of your tongue. Try turning the question back to your child: "I don't know. What do you think?" You might be surprised (and amused) by the response.

ELEMENTARY (AGES 5-10) · · · · · · · · · · · · · · · · · · ·

Penny Walk

Round up your family for a neighborhood stroll and take along a penny. At every corner or intersection, have someone flip the penny. Heads means you turn right, tails means you turn left. You may end up in a place you've never seen before, or you may end up right back at your own house.

Talk about whether flipping a coin is a good way to make decisions. Are there better ways to make choices? What about the big decisions we face? How can God help us when we have a choice that's tough to make? Does God care about all the choices we make all day long? Tell about a time when you needed God's guidance to make a big decision.

Spirit Wind

Kids this age struggle to grasp the concept of the Holy Spirit (as we all do). When you see the wind bending tree branches, compare what you see to the way the Holy Spirit acts in our lives: We can't see the wind, but we can see how it moves the branches. We can't hear the wind, but we can hear the rustling of the leaves as the wind blows through. In the same way, we may not see or hear the Holy Spirit, but we can see evidence of the Spirit's work in our lives when we make good choices or when we feel peace that comes from faith in God.

Scavenger Hunt

Give your kids the following list of items to collect from the back yard or a neighborhood park:

> 1 thorn
> 1 rock
> 1 leaf
> 1 feather
> 1 seed
> a dab of mud

Once they've collected everything on the list, help them think of Bible stories that include these items. Here are some possibilities:

> thorn – Jesus' crown of thorns, or the thorns that choked out faith in the parable of the sower (Matthew 13:18-23)
> rock – the stone that was rolled away from the tomb
> leaf – the palms waved at Jesus' entry into Jerusalem
> feather – God's concern for the tiny sparrow
> seed – faith like a mustard seed
> a dab of mud – the mud Jesus made to heal the blind man

Litter Walk

Living on a street that gets quite a bit of through traffic, the sidewalks close to our house are often decorated with fast-food containers and pop cans. Every now and then when we take one of our walks, we carry along a couple of trash bags to collect the litter as we go—one for throwing away and one for recycling. It's a good way to reinforce our responsibility to care for God's creation, and lessons on forgiveness often make their way into our conversation as well. The kids tend to express their disgust fairly loudly for people who make our street their personal trash can, and I have to say Bruce and I agree with them. But we try to remind one another that we all do things we know we should not do, and that God forgives us every time.

It may work better for your family to visit a local park to do some clean-up. Working together toward a common goal that benefits God's creation will make a big impression on young minds and hearts.

PRETEEN (AGES 10-12) •

Take a Hike

When your children reach the preteen years, it can be a major task to get them off the couch and out the door. If you're battling their fear that someone may discover that they actually enjoy spending time with their parents, it's even more difficult. You may have better luck if you haul your preteen as far away from home as time permits—maybe to a park or hiking trail.

Through Bruce's work for the Girl Scouts of America, we've been blessed with many opportunities to get away close—but not too close—to home. Many weekends when he's teaching troop leaders how to lead zipline and rappel programs, I take the kids out to join him for a hike through the woods. As we tramp up and down hills discovering wild flowers, weird bugs, and the occasional snake, we tend to forget the list of errands that still need doing and the many loads of laundry waiting for us at home. The Holy Spirit tends to take over at these times, lightening our hearts and allowing us to thank God for the great gift of the natural world.

If you're not familiar with natural areas in your community, check your local library or parks and recreation center for suggestions. Even if the only place you can experience nature is a park in the middle of the city, the change of scenery can open up a whole new world to your family. Look for birds you don't see in your yard, or trees that aren't found in your neighborhood. Give thanks for the people who created the park so that you could enjoy God's creation.

Star Gazing

Take advantage of your preteens' later bedtime by spending some time with them staring at the stars. Kids this age are working to grasp enormous concepts, such as eternity, creation, life and death. As you watch the night sky together, it's natural to discuss the immenseness of a God who created the universe, and our place in that creation. You might get the conversation started with open-ended questions such as, "I wonder why God chose this little planet to put people on? What do you think?" Make it your goal to listen more than you talk—give your kids time to think and respond in their own way.

Walk for Charity

Kids in early adolescence often develop a strong sense of concern for others. Help your preteens find an outlet for their generous impulses, praising them for showing Christ-like concern. Many organizations hold sponsored walks to raise funds, and preteens have enough stamina at this age to participate. Make it a joint event and walk together. Suggest that they invite a friend to come along.

Thinking of Layney's concern that our family might get lost and never find our way back home, another idea occurs to me: When we work at our faith and make it our own, we are "at home" no matter where we find ourselves. Our loving God keeps us grounded and secure.

You may be indoors, stuck in a meeting at the office, for example, and struggling to show kindness and mercy to a co-worker with whom you disagree. Or you may be outdoors, witnessing God's intense and particular interest in you and this earth through the beauty of nature. No matter where you are or what you are doing, you have the comfort of being "at home" with God, if you make the effort to live your faith. This is a valuable lesson to teach your kids.

CHAPTER SEVEN

AROUND THE TABLE

You're rich if you've had a meal today.
—*Billy Graham*

Recently I was asked to lead the opening devotion at our church's annual leadership retreat. With my background in elementary education, I enjoy surprising adult groups with activities that are generally considered child-like. Remember, we're only as old as we force ourselves to be! So, instead of going the traditional route and simply reading a Scripture verse with an accompanying reflection, I turned to one of my favorite resources, *How Each Child Learns: Using Multiple Intelligence in Faith Formation* by Bernadette Stankard. This book outlines engaging ways to promote faith development by appealing to the nine intelligences defined by Howard Gardner, professor of education at Harvard. In her chapter on visual-spatial intelligence, Stankard describes an activity called the Mystery Tray, which "forces the group to make connections between the abstract and the concrete."

For this retreat, I had carted along a favorite serving tray from our kitchen, a dish towel, and a toy table from our girls' doll set. Before I greeted the group of thirty church leaders, I had placed the toy table on top of the tray and covered it with the towel. Introducing the game, I laid the ground rules: Participants could not take the towel off the object, but they could ask as many "yes or no" questions as they needed in order to guess what the object was—as long as they took turns asking and listened to each other. (You might be surprised to find that adults need a reminder to listen every bit as much as children do.) It took about ten questions for the group to guess that there was a table on the tray.

With the towel removed and the table exposed, we changed the focus of the activity to a new question: "How is God like a table?" I rejoiced in the answers we heard to that question:

"God is sturdy and solid."
"God gives support."
"God allows room for many."
"A table is for feeding people, just as God feeds us."

Thinking it over later, I realized that these answers are especially true of the tables in our homes. The time we spend around the table as a family creates a sturdy, solid and supportive basis for our lives. When we use our mealtime tables to remind us of those who are hungry and in need, we move in the direction of allowing room for many. And just as our bodies are fed in our daily meals, we can use mealtime to help root our families in faith, receiving the spiritual food provided by God.

INFANT & TODDLER (UP TO AGE 3) . . . .

Finger "Paint"

Your little one's had enough yogurt or pudding, but there's still some left in the cup. Spoon the leftovers onto her high-chair tray and show her how to make designs in the "paint." I know it's messy—Bruce had to convince me to let go of my maternal instinct against playing with our food—but the smiles on your daughter's face will make it worth the mess. Show her how to make a handprint. Write her name inside the print, saying, "See, I have inscribed you on the palms of my hands" (Isaiah 49:16). If they're old enough, they might want to try drawing a cross or the fish symbol.

"Feed Me"

Let your toddler feed you while you're feeding her. It might induce her to eat a little more, and you can talk about God asking us to take care of each other. Thank your child for every bite she gives you (even if it's hard once you get a glimpse of her grimy hands).

Mealtime Prayer

Even the youngest child can learn to fold his hands for the blessing before the meal. Recently while we were babysitting a friend's not-quite-two-year-old child, he joined right in with our family as we folded our hands and bowed our heads for the suppertime prayer. Though the child was too young to fully understand all the words or the meanings behind them, we were all touched by his ability to pause and think about God before he ate.

Before each meal, help toddlers fold their hands to pray with the family. Don't worry if they're noisy or wiggly. Just consider it "making a joyful noise to the Lord" (Psalm 98:4). No matter how irreverent they may seem, rest assured they're learning by your example.

PRESCHOOL (AGES 3-5) •••••••••••••••••••••

Colorful Food

Try putting food coloring in milk or white rice to match the season of
the church year. For example, blue rice during Advent can be a reminder
of the season of waiting and preparing. Or mix some blue and red for
purple milk during Lent and talk about any Lenten practices your family
or church may have. When you get to Easter, white milk and rice will be
back in season.

Mock Manna

Tell your children the story of the Israelites' dependence on manna
in the wilderness. Then place sandwiches, chips, and apple slices into
sandwich baggies and lay them out on various spots on the floor to
be picked up and eaten, like the manna. If the weather cooperates, go
outside and eat on the ground, as the Israelites would have done.

Placemat Art

Keep your preschoolers busy while you're cooking. Ask them to
decorate sheets of paper to use as placemats at supper. Have them draw
pictures of Bible stories, or use simple symbols such as fish, water, or
the cross. While you eat, let them tell the family why they used each
picture or symbol.

"Where Did It Come From?"

Pick a food item on your plate. Discuss where it came from, how many
people must have been involved in getting it to your table. Preschoolers
are fascinated by the thought of the farm animals that give us milk
and eggs, and by the tractors and trucks needed for harvesting and
transportation. Lift up the value of all the different people who do the
jobs required to get our food to us. Say a prayer of thanks for the special
gifts God gave each of those people.

ELEMENTARY (AGES 5-10) · · · · · · · · · · · · · · · · · · ·

Empty Chair

Set an extra place at the table, with an extra chair. Let it be a reminder of Jesus' presence in your midst. You can also use this spot as a reminder of those who aren't with you but who still need your prayers, especially those who don't have the food or family they need.

High Points and Low Points

Supper tends to be the time when the highs and lows of the day come spilling out at our house. Make sure everyone has a chance to share by taking turns, sharing first each person's low points and then each person's high points. Before you leave the table, offer prayers asking God's help with your "lows" and thanking God for your "highs."

Accentuate the Positive

Bruce and I find that our family members tend to be more short-tempered and critical of each other during supper. We seem to have a need to let out the day's trials, and we often lash out at those closest to us. Sometimes a moment of silence is called for. We suggest that each person in our family think of one positive quality of the person sitting next to them. After that think time, we share those qualities. ("She's not as stupid as she was yesterday" doesn't count.) You might follow up the exercise with a discussion of looking for Christ in all people, even those with whom we have difficulties.

Making Do

My suppertime angst is often a direct result of trying to come up with an edible meal when we're desperately due for a trip to the grocery store. Bruce is especially good at making something out of nothing, so I try to hand the cooking reins over to him on these days. Then we use the "out of groceries" discussion to remind our kids of what Jesus said in Matthew 6:25: "Do not worry about…what you will eat or what you will drink." It's a good lesson for us all, as comfortable and well-fed as we are.

Your children may enjoy taking on the task of "making supper out of nothing" themselves. Give them free rein, and try not to grimace if what they come up with turns out to be pancakes and canned baked beans. Together you can work toward appreciation of whatever food God provides.

ABC's of Blessings

Throughout the meal, play this game: The first person says, "A: I'm thankful for the applesauce (or avocados or air)." The second person goes on with, "B: I'm thankful for bread (or beef or a new ball glove)," and so on. The list might get a little silly, especially with Q and Z, but it will help everyone in your family remember how infinite your blessings really are.

Blessing Jar

Keep a jar (or a bowl or a basket) on the kitchen or dining room table, with a pad and pencil nearby. Invite everyone to jot down anything that happened during the day for which they're especially thankful. Challenge the family to fill the jar by suppertime. As you eat, take turns pulling out notes and reading them aloud.

"No Dessert?"

If you can stand the complaints that are likely to ensue, deliberately leave dessert out of the family supper plans for a week or so. Use the experiment to highlight the difference between wants and needs. Discuss ways that God cares for our needs. Note the fact that many people throughout the world require help just to have their most basic needs met and must do without frills like dessert. Point out to your kids that God calls us to love and help these neighbors. This activity is especially appropriate during Lent, but it can be done throughout the year.

PRETEEN (AGES 10-12) ●●●●●●●●●●●●●●●●●●●●●●

"Where in the World?"

Friends of ours kept a world map hanging near their dinner table. It is a great way to spark discussions about different people around the world, as well as increasing everyone's geographic I.Q. You might also use the map to compare foods eaten in different parts of the world, to highlight places where people regularly go without sufficient food, and to help your family remember to pray for those who are in need.

Dine by Candlelight

Ask your preteens to write a simple prayer to share at supper about light and darkness. Then turn off all electric lights and eat with only candles lit. Mention that Jesus and his disciples must have eaten by candlelight often. Ask your kids to pay attention to the brightness of the candlelight in the darkness of the room and then compare it to the light Jesus brings to the world.

"Is That All?"

With the growth spurts they're experiencing, preteens tend to have enormous appetites. Surprise your sons or daughters by serving extremely small portions one night (but be prepared to dish up seconds later on). Ask them what it feels like not to get enough food. Consider the petition for daily bread in the Lord's Prayer. Help them understand that when Jesus instructed us to pray, "Give us this day our daily bread," he was referring to everyone, everywhere, and that as we say the Lord's Prayer we are praying for all the needy of the world, not just for ourselves.

Salt of the Earth

Deliberately leave all salt out of a dish you cook for supper. One taste should be enough to elicit comments about the blandness of the meal. Discuss Jesus' pronouncement that we are the salt of the earth. Ask your preteens to consider what salt does for our food. They'll probably point out that it makes food better. Ask them how they personally can help make things better for the world.

As important as it is for us to eat together regularly, there are nights when one or more of us can't be there for supper. Bruce could tell you how stressed and crabby I get when our time around the table is taken away from us by outside commitments. I consider that time of gathering to be vital to our family's health and well-being, and I tend to overreact when it's taken away. So when we are all together around the table, whether that table is in our dining room or at the fast-food place that's closest to our evening commitments, it's important that we use the time to its fullest potential.

You know how easy it is to get caught up in day-to-day issues and lose sight of what a blessing it is even to have food on your table. When you can focus on your gratitude for the tremendous blessings of food, family and home, mealtime can become a time of growing faith for every member of your family.

CHAPTER EIGHT

BEDTIME

The bed is a bundle of paradoxes:
we go to it with reluctance, yet we quit it with regret;
we make up our minds every night to leave it early,
but we make up our bodies every morning to keep it late.
—*Ogden Nash*

"Bedtime" is a bad word for many children. And their reaction to the suggestion of going to bed can cause parents to utter their own bad words. I recall one disastrous bedtime experience when our second daughter was about two years old. Bruce was at a meeting, and I was on bedtime duty all by myself. Our oldest, Kayla, was in bed and sound asleep seconds after her head hit the pillow. I knew better than to expect the same from her little sister, a reluctant sleeper from birth. I tucked Layney in, arranged her blankets and stuffed animals to specification, gave her a drink of water, sang her numerous songs and tiptoed downstairs. She hopped out of bed and followed me. I took her back to bed and returned downstairs. Moments later she was tugging at my shirt. We repeated this scene a total of seventeen times that evening. I counted. I thank God that a friend phoned during tuck-in number seven, just as I was about to lose control. The phone call was a lifeline that distracted me from the maddening situation at hand and helped me retain my humor.

I was thankful, too, for the presence of the Holy Spirit that evening, which wrapped me in grace and allowed me to share that grace with my persistent daughter. Though I wanted nothing more than to curl up with a cup of hot tea and a good book, the Spirit helped me pray my way through the many trips up and down the stairs, through the many visits to the rocking chair, through the lullabies I repeated for what seemed like hours.

As hard as it is to be patient at bedtime, when we're worn out from a long day of working (whether in the home or outside of it) and parenting, it's important to try to understand the struggle kids go through at bedtime. If it's not dark outside yet, it soon will be. And there's a whole imaginary world of frightening things out there in the dark. For younger children it might be monsters in the closet. For older kids it could be fear of a disaster that could harm their family or their home. Even for adults, any little trouble or worry that's been nagging at us throughout the day stretches to exaggerated proportions after the sun goes down.

We all need the reassurance of God's love and care for us at that dark hour of bedtime. It's a true comfort to know that even when we're asleep and dreaming, God "will neither slumber or sleep" (Psalm 121:4). I hope the activities in this chapter will help you share that message with your children every night.

INFANT & TODDLER (UP TO AGE 3) . . . .

Decorating the Nursery

Part of the excitement and anticipation of a new baby in the family is decorating the baby's bedroom. As parents, we put a lot of thought into just the right colors, furniture and toys. Often, though, we're looking at the room from an aesthetic view point only. Cute and cozy is our main consideration.

Since children spend so many hours in their rooms, it's important to include reminders of our faith in the decorative touches. Display mementoes of your baby's baptism. When our youngest was baptized, the pastor dipped the water from the font with a seashell, which now sits on a shelf in Garrett's room. Place a cross on the wall. Frame a picture of Noah's Ark or Jesus and the children. Your baby will fall asleep each night and awake each morning looking at visual reminders of your faith.

Hold that Baby

Bruce and I never bought into the warnings that we would spoil our babies if we held them too much. During that short, golden time when we were the parents of an infant, toddler and preschooler, there was rarely a time when one of us didn't have a child in our arms, on our shoulders, or sitting on our laps.

When we hold our children in our arms, we help them recognize the loving arms of God that are wrapped around them as well. If a child has experienced the loving arms of a parent, it's not much of a cognitive leap to understand God's ever-present arms. Hold that baby or toddler as much as you can, before your child gets distracted by the world and runs off to grow up!

Rock-a-bye Baby

Rocking your infant or toddler before bed is a natural. That last intimate connection with Mommy or Daddy before bed soothes, reassures, and, we hope, helps our little ones to nod off. Singing a quiet lullabye while you rock can help those wide eyes start to close. Send them off to sleep with a soft rendition of "Jesus Loves Me" or "Away in a Manger" (our kids asked for this Christmas song year-round). They'll love the sound of your voice whether you can carry a tune or not. Lose your inhibitions—after all, you've only got an audience of one and your child is not exactly discerning at this age. Your soft voice and loving arms will echo God's love.

Baptism and Bath Water

For many families, bath time signals the end of the day and the beginning of bedtime. The warm water of a bath soothes and comforts, helping children calm down and (we hope) get ready to sleep. If your faith tradition celebrates infant baptism, your preschoolers are old enough to begin to understand this concept. When you have them in the tub, tell them the story of their baptism. Explain how water was poured onto their heads as a promise that Jesus would watch over them forever as children of God.

Sign of the Cross

A friend of ours has a bedtime ritual that began when her children were very young. When tucking them in and saying prayers, she traces the sign of the cross on their foreheads. Consider using this reminder of baptism with your children. Your gentle touch can remind them of Jesus' watch over all their hours, both awake and asleep.

Bedtime Bible Stories

Bedtime stories have always been a part of our family's nightly routine. When our oldest turned three and received her first story Bible, we started including biblical stories. Every night each child was allowed to choose one story from the Bible. It didn't matter to us that one invariably chose the story of the treasure and the pearl (Matthew 13:44-46), and another insisted nightly on the angel appearing to Mary to announce the coming of Jesus (Luke 1:28-38). Young children thrive on repetition and predictability. Every night they were assured God's word would stay the same. Isn't that what we all need?

Many times when we plant these seeds in our children, we feel we may never see them come to fruition. Recently, though, Bruce and I were blessed to observe the results of our bedtime Bible story tradition. Our children feel they've outgrown their picture Bible story books, but each of them now has a student Bible. One night after prayers and tucking in, Garrett called me into his room. He had his Bible out and wanted to know where to find the story of Jesus' death and resurrection. We took great joy in knowing our son wanted to read God's word.

Family Prayer

This is a perfect age to model the importance of prayer. Build a bedtime prayer into your nightly routine. Rhyming prayers are easy for young children to remember and recite with you. (There are suggestions for simple rhyming prayers at the end of this chapter.) Conclude your prayer time by naming things you're thankful for on this particular day, or with petitions for friends or family who are on your mind.

Sometimes parents are uncomfortable with their children's prayer concerns. We may feel silly praying for a child's stuffed animal or giving thanks for the chocolate ice cream we had for dessert. Keep in mind that God wants us to pray about everything—every single, little thing—and allow your children to lead the way with their uninhibited prayers. Surely God appreciates the faith and trust these prayers demonstrate. Remember Jesus' words in Matthew 18:3: "Truly I tell you, unless you change and become like children, you will never enter the kingdom of heaven."

Play It Again, and Again, and Again

Preschoolers demand routine. Cater to this need for safety and predictability by following, as closely as possible, the same bedtime rituals every night. Not only will this be a comfort for your kids, but you may also find some peace in knowing that your hectic day will end the same way every evening.

Your four year old may feel he's outgrown rocking and singing at bedtime, but music is still an effective sleep-inducing tool. Find a CD of faith-based lullabies. Buy him an inexpensive, simply-operated CD player and teach him how to turn it on and off. Our son, Garrett, had a hard time winding down at night and often needed to play his bedtime music several times through before he drifted off. Being able to re-play the music on his own gave him a small sense of control and eliminated our running up and down the stairs every twenty-five minutes. And the sound of him singing "Angels Watching over Me" along with his CD was music to our ears.

ELEMENTARY (AGES 5-10) • • • • • • • • • • • • • • • • • •

Keep Reading

As they grow, children may think they've become too old for stories at bedtime. As a former teacher, however, I've seen first-hand how important it is for families to keep reading together. Not only does family reading time foster a love of books and life-long learning, but it also provides fertile ground for discussion. Share with your children books such as the "Narnia Chronicles" by C. S. Lewis and the "Time Quartet" by Madeleine L'Engle, starting with *A Wrinkle in Time*. Both authors embrace faith-related themes in stories that appeal to children's interests. See the list of books at the end of this chapter for suggestions of faith-filled bedtime stories for all ages.

Thankfulness Books

Friends of ours have created a unique bedtime tradition with their children. Each family member has his or her own notebook to write in, and every night they spend a few minutes writing about what they're thankful for.

Supply each member of your family with a spiral notebook to use for their own thankfulness book. As you add to it, you'll create an attitude of appreciation for God's blessings. And you'll all have a record you can look back on to remind you of what you felt was important at any given time in your lives.

Update your Prayers

School-age children may be outgrowing the simple, rhyming bedtime prayers you established when they were younger. They're old enough now to learn the Lord's Prayer. Try saying it together, pausing between phrases to add your own petitions. C. S. Lewis called this practice "praying with festoons," and it's an effective way to bring form and meaning to your nightly prayers. For example:

"Our Father in heaven, hallowed be your name…"
> Thank you, God, for taking care of us like a father.

"Your kingdom come, your will be done, on earth as it is in heaven…"
> Help me to do what you want me to do here on earth.
> Help me to_____.

"Give us this day our daily bread…"
> Please give us everything we need,
> and please help (name friends' needs)

"Forgive us our debts as we also have forgiven our debtors…"
> I'm sorry for _____. Please forgive me.
> Help me forgive _____.

"And do not bring us to the time of trial,
but rescue us from the evil one …"
> Help me with _____ and keep me safe.

More Music

As children grow older, they're faced with more stress than we may realize. Homework, hormones and relationships start to tower over them. These concerns weigh especially heavily on the kids' minds at bedtime, sometimes keeping them from being able to fall asleep.

Though children in this age group are unlikely to enjoy lullabies, faith-based music can be a good tool for helping them deal with the kinds of concerns that might keep them awake at night. On an occasion when our daughter was having a rough night, Bruce produced his personal CD player, a set of headphones, and a CD of her favorite Scriptural-based music (recorded by our church's youth band). She played the CD through a couple of times before she relaxed enough to fall asleep, but the experiment was a distinct success. Now she has her own player and headphones. When your child is having a rough time—day or night—help her turn to music to put herself back on track with a reminder of God's promises.

PRETEEN (AGES 10-12) ••••••••••••••••••••

Night Owls

When our daughter Kayla started middle school, her homework load took a huge, burdensome leap. Many nights she was at it from the time she got home from school until bedtime, with only a break for supper. But going straight from homework to bed took a toll pretty quickly. Bruce and I did what we could to build in some down time for Kayla before she went to bed. With her siblings already asleep, we made a point of spending some quiet time alone with her several nights a week. (It was easy for my husband, who is naturally nocturnal. My motor, however, starts to sputter soon after sundown. Often Kayla had to nudge me awake to play a game of cards with her after the homework was done.)

Those few minutes of one-on-one time at the end of the day can be a big step toward keeping your relationship with your preteen alive and growing. And keeping that relationship alive is a vital part of helping them expand their relationship with Christ.

Nighttime Notes

If you find that your formerly chatty preteen has become nearly nonverbal, try note-writing as a way to communicate with them. Write a note of encouragement and leave it on his pillow to read before going to bed. Mention things you've noticed that make you proud. Include actions he's taken that reflect Jesus' love. Leave no doubt that you are one-hundred percent on his side and that you expect great things from him. Everyone needs to know that there's someone who stands with us through the trials of life. As parents, we're the best example our children are going to get of God's love here on Earth.

Turn your note writing into weekly habit, and before long you may find a note on your own pillow.

Prime-Time Viewing

Discussion of the quality of television programming is a constant today. Between many organizations lobbying for more family-friendly shows and television producers pandering to the lowest common denominator, there's a wealth of conversation opportunities about the "tube." Make a point of watching some of the more popular prime time shows with your preteen. For example, reality shows often send a message that we must be beautiful, wealthy, "perfect" in order to get ahead and be happy. Contrast this messages with the lessons Jesus wants us to learn. Ask your preteen thoughtful questions, such as, "What can you take away from the show that will help you be a better person?" "What things in the program might affect you negatively?" "How do you think the message of this program fits in (or doesn't fit) with God's message to us?"

When our kids were very young, we used to be so worn out by their bedtime we couldn't wait to get them to sleep. Bruce and I were pretty strict about early bedtime, since those short minutes after they were out for the night were our only time alone together. At the same time, we looked forward every morning to the joy of seeing their bright smiles peeping at us over the crib bars. Using some of the suggestions in this chapter helped us survive the bedtime struggle, allow quiet time for ourselves, and appreciate our precious children—even on those "seventeen tuck-in" nights.

Help your children appreciate the gift of sleep God gives us each night. They—and you—need the time to rest so you start again, refreshed and ready for a new day, a new chance to live a day of faith.

BEDTIME PRAYERS •••••••••••••••••••••••••

Now I lay me down to sleep,
I pray the Lord my soul to keep.
Love and watch me through the night,
And wake me with the morning light.

Jesus, watch me while I sleep.
Your loving arms around me keep.

Thank you, God, for this day,
For times to work and times to play,
For family, friends, and all I see,
Thank you, God, for loving me.

Now the night is coming,
Stars are overhead.
Jesus, watch and keep me,
Safe within my bed.

Jesus, stay beside me,
Always watching over me,
Help me know you love me,
All the night and day.

FAITH-FILLED BEDTIME STORIES ••••••••••••••

A bedtime story routine does more than bring the family together for a quiet, cozy time to wind down at the end of the day. It can also provide a time to discuss good literature and reflect on how it relates to your faith.

When choosing bedtime stories, remember that any good book has something to say to us, no matter what our age. It's okay to read a picture book to your grade-schooler. Try a chapter book with your five-year-old. Share a book you loved as a child with your preteen and tell why it meant so much to you. It's the caring, thoughtful conversation that takes place around the reading that makes a book come alive.

The Beginner's Bible, ZonderKidz.
> A simple retelling of the Bible, beginning with Genesis and continuing through Revelation. Lively and fun illustrations.

The Best Christmas Pageant Ever, Barbara Robinson, HarperCollins.
> A chapter book, perfect for December bedtime reading, that illustrates how the most unlikely messengers can tell us about God's love for us.

The Complete Chronicles of Narnia, C. S. Lewis, HarperCollins.
> The seven Narnia tales, from "The Magician's Nephew" to "The Last Battle," explore themes of good vs. evil, salvation and unconditional love through action and adventure. (Perhaps you might want to tie your reading in with seeing the movie editions.)

The Giving Tree, Shel Silverstein, HarperCollins.
> A picture book with a poignant story of selfless love.

Horton Hears a Who, Dr. Seuss, Random House.
> A picture book with Dr. Seuss's distinct style of illustration and verse that teaches the value of every individual, no matter how small or seemingly insignificant.

Love You Forever, Robert N. Munsch, Firefly Books.
A picture book that follows the loving, enduring relationship of a parent and child from infancy to adulthood.

Many Waters, Madeleine L'Engle, Farrar, Straus and Giroux.
A time-travel fantasy that illustrates the world in the time of Noah, with themes of good vs. evil and God's plan for each of us. (Book Four of L'Engle's "Time Quartet")

Ramona Quimby, Age 8, Beverly Cleary, Dell.
A chapter book dealing with the ups and downs of living within a family and learning to appreciate the family we have.

Read-Aloud Bible Stories, Ella K. Lindvall, Moody Publishers.
A four-volume picture book of favorite Old and New Testament stories retold through very simple, rhythmic language. Large, vivid illustrations.

The Runaway Bunny, Margaret Wise Brown, HarperCollins.
A picture book depicting the loving relationship between a parent and child that will not be broken no matter where the child may wander.

A Swiftly Tilting Planet, Madeleine L'Engle, Farrar, Straus and Giroux.
A time-travel fantasy with themes of good vs. evil and the importance of tolerance and understanding. (Book Two of L'Engle's "Time Quartet")

A Wind in the Door, Madeleine L'Engle, Farrar, Straus and Giroux.
A continuation of the cosmic battle between good and evil, with emphasis on the interconnectedness of all things. (Book Three of the L'Engle's "Time Quartet")

A Wrinkle in Time, Madeleine L'Engle, Farrar, Straus and Giroux.
This classic time-travel fantasy deals with themes from self-concept and fitting in, to the all-powerful gift of love. (Book One of L'Engle's "Time Quartet")

CHAPTER NINE

SPECIAL OCCASIONS

Shared joy is double joy.
Shared sorrow is half sorrow.
—*Swedish Proverb*

Families can be a tremendous blessing in times of joy and sorrow. We celebrate together in happy times; we support and pray for each other when life becomes hard. I hate to think how empty our days would be without family, both nuclear and extended.

A couple of years ago, on Palm Sunday, Kayla fell and broke her arm while we were on a family bike ride. Truthfully, "broke" doesn't begin to describe what happened. Two bones were completely shattered. Her arm looked as if it were made of melted rubber. I still get a cold chill remembering the unnatural curve in her forearm.

Together we made it through the ambulance ride, the emergency room visit, and a grisly (but failed) attempt to set her arm. The pediatric orthopedic surgeon decided surgery was required, and the date was set for Good Friday. The darkness of this holiest of days seemed especially appropriate that year.

There was a five-hour wait once we got to the hospital on the morning of Good Friday. Five hours, of course, with no food or drink for our little girl (or Bruce and me, either, as we couldn't bear to eat or drink in front of her). When they finally wheeled her off to the operating room, we were told to expect the surgery to last about an hour. Three anxious, frightening hours later the surgeon came out to tell us about the various pins, screws and plates she'd had to use to repair Kayla's bones.

While I wouldn't care to relive the experience, its memory holds a warmth and comfort that have served to strengthen our faith. It came from the many friends at church and in our neighborhood who held us in prayer, and from the family members who jumped in to help. Kayla's aunt, uncle and cousins left work and school early that Good Friday and drove four hours so they could pick up her siblings from school while we were at the hospital. They fed all the kids and took them to church that evening. They stayed for the weekend and helped with child care, cooking, even ironing—now that's true love! They were there to celebrate with us both Kayla's return home and Jesus' resurrection that Easter Sunday.

Because extended family gatherings—whether in crisis or celebration—are multi-generational, the faith-building activities in this chapter are categorized by occasion rather than by age. At our family gatherings, we've found that older relatives enjoy the chance to try activities that seem child-like. Younger cousins like to feel important as they join in with the folks who get to sit at the "grown-up table." Just as we adults can learn from the simple faith of a child, our children can benefit from faith stories told by their elders.

Think about which special event your family is likely to celebrate together next, and see which suggestions for that event might fit your family. May God bless your efforts to turn the occasion into a time of faith-building.

BIRTHDAYS ••••••••••••••••••••••••••••••

Add a Verse

After the traditional off-key rendering of "Happy Birthday," add this second verse to remind the birthday boy or girl of God's presence in the celebration:

> May the dear Lord bless you,
> May the dear Lord keep you,
> May the dear Lord watch o'er you
> We thank God for you.

Give Thanks, Make a Wish

Add an extra ritual to the blowing out of birthday candles. Right after making a wish, have the birthday boy or girl announce one thing to be grateful for, then proceed to blow out the candles.

"I Thank God for You"

Sometimes the most special gift costs nothing at all. Our daughter, Layney, has been blessed with creative and artistic skills. One of her handmade gifts or cards is the highlight of any celebration in our family. Even if you're as artistically challenged as Bruce and I are, your family can create an "I Thank God for You" card.

Have someone in the family decorate the front of a homemade card, either on construction paper or on the computer. On the inside, each member of the family writes one or more reasons why they thank God for the birthday person. Sisters and brothers, aunts and uncles, and grandparents alike appreciate the thought and love behind an "I Thank God for You" card.

Family Photos

We love to take out our photo albums on our children's birthdays to help us remember exactly what we were feeling when the birthday boy or girl came into our lives.

When we get together for birthdays of aunts, cousins or grandparents, older photos can spark valuable storytelling opportunities. Take the time to listen to these stories and encourage the storytellers to include details about their faith lives. Ask what church activities they were involved with at the time of each photo. Encourage them to tell about how their faith helped them through difficult times.

In our family of stoic northern-European ancestry, this kind of discussion doesn't always come naturally. You may find, as well, that it can be hard for family members to share about their faith journeys at first. But it's worth a little bit of gentle prodding to learn the history of your family's faith.

Turn-Around Gifts

When your children are old enough to see beyond themselves (and that age differs widely from child to child), suggest that they request "turn-around" gifts from their friends for a birthday party. For a winter birthday, they could ask their guests to bring a pair of gloves or a scarf to be donated to a relief agency, instead of another action figure or doll that will end up on the closet floor. For a summer birthday, they might request donations of non-perishable foods (food pantries often see a decline in support during the hot months).

The concept of turn-around gifts may require a fair amount of discussion and education beforehand. Some children may never be ready for such a gesture, and that's okay. They'll find other ways of sharing with their neighbors, with your guidance.

If turn-around gifting is to be a possibility, it's important first to cultivate a family attitude of thankfulness for blessings and a concern for those less fortunate. You can assure your child she will still receive birthday presents from her family. But you can also help her keep in mind that bringing items for the needy will provide her friends with an opportunity for giving they might not otherwise have. As she follows Jesus' example of caring for our neighbors, she might be planting a seed in others to do the same.

Baptismal Anniversaries

We celebrate infant baptism in our faith tradition, and our children's baptismal dates are close to their birthdays. No matter when the anniversary of a baptism occurs, it's an opportune time to gather the family and give thanks that this person is forever a child of God. You might consider looking through pictures of the baptismal day, lighting your child's baptismal candle, or simply writing your child a brief note to encourage his faith.

Calendar Review

Before you throw out the previous year's calendar, gather the family together to look over the entries you made on it throughout the year. You'll find dates of parties, dance recitals, doctor appointments, and many other events both big and small. Say a prayer of thanks for all the wonderful things you were able to do last year, for your family's health, and for the talents you've all been given.

A Different Spin on New Year's Resolutions

Ask the members of your family to think of one thing they would like to change about their relationship with God. Perhaps they might want to give God more thanks, or pray more often, or remember to love as God taught us. Whatever it is, they don't have to share it with the rest of the family—this resolution is between themselves and God. Then together ask God to help each of you make those changes. Finally, give thanks for the assurance that if we fail, as we so often do, we'll be forgiven and receive the grace to try again.

LENT/HOLY WEEK/EASTER ••••••••••••••••••••

Prayer Journal

The season of Lent is a time to try out new spiritual practices that remind us of Jesus' sacrifice. A commitment to daily prayer is a good Lenten discipline, but it can be hard to take time for prayer. If the whole family is involved, you can help one another. Try using a family prayer journal throughout the weeks of Lent. You could buy an attractive journal, or just grab a spiral notebook or a notepad out of a drawer. It doesn't matter what your journal looks like—the important thing is to use it.

Discuss the best time of day for your family to come together, then decide together how you want your prayer journal to work. You might want to make it a "thankfulness journal," in which you list your blessings each day. Or you might let each family member take turns writing down prayer concerns. There will be days when everyone forgets, or when you simply don't have time to write in the journal. Don't get discouraged, and don't give up. Remind your kids that God gives us a fresh chance every day to renew our commitments.

Bury the Alleluias

Traditionally, the church has omitted the celebratory "Alleluia" in worship throughout the weeks of Lent. Lent is a time of reflection to remember the greatness of God's act of love in sending Jesus to straighten out our messy lives and pay for our sins. For a concrete way to help your family focus on the sober, thoughtful nature of the Lenten season, try the following activity:

Write the word "alleluia" on sheets of paper. (Despite my comments in the introduction about "rounding up supplies," this is a time when you might want to use brightly colored markers or crayons and add your own creative touches. But you can always use any old piece of paper, and the only sharpened pencil you can find. The message will get through either way.)

Have the kids help you fold up the papers and bury them at the bottom of the messiest drawers or closets in the house. (If your house is like ours, you'll have several to choose from!) Tell your kids that the clutter symbolizes the messiness and mistakes we all have in our lives.

Then go to the calendar and make a note to remind you all to take your Alleluias out of hiding on Easter Sunday.

Palm Parade

If your church has a procession with palms on the Sunday before Easter, take your palms home with you and display them in a visible spot. Some night during Holy Week, before bedtime, hold a Palm Parade. Go through the house, stopping at each room for a loud "hosanna" and a prayer of thanks. Stop at different rooms in the house for a brief prayer of thanksgiving. In the kitchen, you can thank God for providing the food your family needs to grow and be strong. In the family room, give thanks for times you play together. End the parade at the bedrooms with a bedtime prayer, keeping in mind that the parade for Jesus led to his crucifixion and resurrection for all of us.

Servant for a Week

Jesus modeled servanthood when he washed the disciples' feet before the Passover Feast: "So if I, your Lord and Teacher, have washed your feet, you also ought to wash one another's feet" (John 13:14). One way to bring this example home is to become servants for a week. On Palm Sunday, have each person in the family draw the name of another family member. Throughout Holy Week, each member of the family looks for concrete ways to serve the person whose name was drawn, without making a big deal about it.

Easter Symbols

Who doesn't want to color eggs or imagine the Easter bunny hiding them in the night? Go ahead and observe these secular aspects of the holiday, but put a spin on them that brings to mind your faith. As you color or hide Easter eggs, talk about what comes out of eggs. A newly-hatched chick, all fuzzy and beautiful, can remind us of the way Jesus makes us new and beautiful by taking away all our sin. The surprise of candy and gifts in an Easter basket can remind us of the amazing surprise Mary Magdelene found when the stone was rolled away from the tomb and Jesus was no longer there.

BACK TO SCHOOL ●

End-of-Summer Wrap-Up

Every year on the evening of the last day before school starts, our family gathers for a pizza supper. As we eat, we make a written list of things we did over the summer. They may be as big as a cross-country trip or as small as weekly visits to the swimming pool. It's our way of celebrating the time we've enjoyed together and committing it to our memories.

You can use this activity to help your family celebrate the time you've enjoyed together. Stash the lists away in a safe place every year. Then you can enjoy getting out lists from summers past and talking over old memories. Make a point of thanking God for giving you those special times.

Surplus School Supplies

A big part of the back-to-school adventure is purchasing new supplies. Starting off a school year with a fresh, clean supply box and pristine folders and notebooks makes the beginning of school an exciting occasion. When I was teaching in the elementary schools, I often saw sadness or embarrassment in children who came to school with broken, stubby crayons and tattered notebooks. It may seem like a small thing to an adult, but it's a major concern for a child.

With school supplies so heavily discounted at back-to-school time, encourage your children to pick out supplies to give to the poor. Help them imagine how it would feel to attend the first day of school with old, worn-out things—or with no supplies at all. Remind them of Jesus' commandment that we are to love our neighbors as ourselves.

Many stores have school supply donation sites at this time of year. If you don't see a collection bin, there's a good chance your school principal will know of someone at your school who's in need of supplies. When we've given supplies to our school in the past, Bruce and I have been touched by our kids' concern for their fellow students. They make a point of choosing the prettiest folders and coolest pencils to give away.

One word of caution: Make sure your children understand how important it is that they keep this act of giving to themselves. By elementary school-age, they should be able to put themselves in others' shoes. They can imagine how uncomfortable they would feel if the whole class knew their family couldn't afford to buy school supplies. And they can understand Jesus' words in Matthew 6:3-4, "When you give alms, do not let your left hand know what your right hand is doing, so that your alms may be done in secret."

THANKSGIVING ●

Scrapbook of Thanks

One year at Thanksgiving, our nephew came home from school with a handmade scrapbook full of empty pages. At our big family meal, everyone in attendance was invited to write on a page, telling about something they felt was special about Thanksgiving and something for which they were thankful. This simple school project gave each of us a chance to consider how richly we'd been blessed.

You might choose to create your own scrapbook, or you could simply use an old spiral notebook. The thoughts that go inside are much more important than any aesthetic qualities.

Circle of Questions

One year for a family Thanksgiving dinner, we typed out questions and slipped them under the dinner plates. The questions ranged from "What would you like to be doing ten years from now?" to "If you could create one law that the entire nation had to abide by, what would it be?" We were careful to put simpler questions under the plates of the younger family members, such as "What's your favorite holiday and why?"

As we sat down to eat, we read silently the questions under our plates (whispering the pre-readers' questions to them). We thought about our answers throughout the meal. Then, when we were finished eating, we took turns reading and answering our questions out loud.

We learned a great deal from each other that day, especially when a friend at our gathering, who had been born and raised in Tanzania, read his question: "Tell about your favorite toy as a child." His answer was that no one he knew as a child had any manufactured toys. He described attempts to make toys out of found materials, and the fun he had with these homemade items. All of us, including the children, were sobered to realize how many blessings God has given us and how much we take for granted.

At your next Thanksgiving celebration, think ahead of time about the people who will gather together. Spend a few minutes—or ask your children to spend a few minutes—writing out questions that will spark interesting conversation among guests. As you discuss the answers after dinner, you may find this time of sharing a blessing for all.

Away in a Manger

Since our oldest was tiny, we've made a big occasion out of singing "Away in a Manger" and placing the baby Jesus in the manger scene before we go to bed on Christmas Eve. The baby in our set isn't wrapped in swaddling cloths, as described in Luke; he's wearing only a scrap of something around his bottom. From an early age, Kayla found his near-naked state distressing. She wore fleecy, footed pajamas to go to bed under thick, warm blankets, but poor baby Jesus had only a tiny piece of cloth. So our Christmas Eve ritual now includes wrapping the little Jesus tightly in a piece of facial tissue (it was the first thing we could find, and the tradition stuck). Giving our attention to this detail of the nativity as our last act on Christmas Eve helps us remember why we celebrate.

Make a point of finding a nativity set that is unbreakable but still attractive, so you don't have to worry when the kids wrap and re-wrap the baby or endlessly rearrange the wise men and animals. You want a manger scene that your children can manipulate and make their own.

Scale Back

Every year Bruce and I swore to each other that we'd cut way back on Christmas craziness and focus on the real message. And every year we ended up in a frenzy, trying to buy just the right gifts for everyone on our list. Until last year. Last year, various circumstances forced us to cut back on many of our holiday preparations. When we realized time and resources were running short, we had to make some changes.

Seemingly out of the blue (though I suspect the Spirit was at work), we thought of some great presents we could make by hand. We went to work and spent much of December creating blankets, bookmarks, ornaments, and spiced tea for our friends and family. The many evenings we spent laughing and working together, looking forward to the giving of these unique gifts, created memories we'll always treasure.

As it turned out, we experienced two deaths in our family the week before Christmas. Other years this sad turn of events in the midst of the holiday rush might have been disastrous. But because we'd been given the blessing of a scaled-back holiday, Bruce and I had the strength and energy to handle our grief and help the kids through it as well.

Next December, I'll be praying for the same Spirit-filled holiday experience we had last year. Consider taking a fresh look at your own Christmas traditions, and think about how they might be scaled back or eliminated. You may be surprised to discover that it's really true—"less is more!"

TIMES OF SORROW •

Get into Action

When someone we love has a health crisis or experiences the death of a loved one, we pray, we visit, but we may feel helpless. Children, especially, can end up feeling powerless when even their most trusted adults seem to be at a loss. One way to get through these difficult times is to get busy. Following Christ's example of servanthood, find ways to serve those who are ill or grieving. Younger children can draw pictures or make cards. Older children can join a family effort to help with housework or yard work. The whole family can work together to prepare and serve a meal. Together, in your acts of servanthood and love, you'll work your way through the difficult time.

My Friend Jesus

We can take comfort in the knowledge that Jesus understands the pain we feel at the death of a loved one. When Jesus' good friend Lazarus became very sick and finally died, Jesus was so sad that he cried (John 11:35).

We can remind our children that Jesus wants them to know he's their good friend, that he wants to be with them when they sit down to eat, when they're talking and playing, and when they're sad. Tell them that when they keep Jesus' love inside their hearts he's right there with them, even in the sad times.

Here's one way you can approach this: Ask your children to imagine playing their favorite game with their best friend. What would they talk about? What kinds of things would they do? Now ask them to imagine Jesus as that best friend, playing the game with them. Imagine that they can talk with him and can even reach out and touch him. How would Jesus play the game? What kinds of things would Jesus say? What would they say to him? Would he laugh when they act silly or tell a joke? Ask your children to tell you what having Jesus for a friend would be like.

Then help your children see that Jesus is right beside them in this sad time too. If they will be attending the funeral of a loved one, tell them that Jesus will sit beside them and cry with them. When they miss the person who has died, Jesus will hold them in his arms and comfort them.

This imagery will help your children know Jesus as a constant, everpresent friend. Sharing such thoughts can help you in your grieving as well.

When we reminisce, it is the special occasions of life that tend to stand out. "Wasn't that the year we went to your sister's house for Christmas?" "That was the summer Aunt Betty died." "Remember that Easter when it was so warm we had a picnic?" These are the times that season our lives like salt.

It is often through extreme highs and lows that faith finds room to grow. Whether you're filled with laughter as you enjoy your favorite holidays together or crying as you mourn the death of a loved one, any of the special occasions in life can be an opportunity to help your family grow in faith.

CHAPTER TEN

FAITH: A GOOD HABIT TO GET INTO

Moral excellence comes about as a result of habit.
We become just by doing just acts,
temperate by doing temperate acts,
brave by doing brave acts.
—Aristotle

Personally, I don't have any grand expectations of attaining moral excellence. I'm doing pretty well if I manage not to do lasting damage to the world around me on any given day. But I believe Aristotle had it right when it comes to habits. Bruce and I want our family to develop a habit of faith. And the only way for faith to become a habit is to do faithful acts.

Experts say that in order for an act to become a habit we must perform it regularly for anywhere from two weeks to three months. I have a feeling the higher number of repetitions is required more for developing good habits than bad; bad habits seem to be infinitely easier to acquire. As Paul put it, "I can will what is right, but I cannot do it. For I do not do the good I want, but the evil I do not want is what I do" (Romans 7:18-19). It's comforting to know we aren't alone in our struggles to build good habits of faith.

Take a moment to consider one of your family's habits. It could be letting the dog out first thing in the morning. Or brushing your teeth before you go to bed (not such a good example in our family—the tooth brushing requirement comes as a complete surprise to our son every night of the week). Whatever that habit is, it's something you all do without thinking. Why? Because you've done it for so long you don't need to think about it any more.

And that's what it takes for our faith to become a living, active part of our daily lives. We just have to do it over and over, on a regular basis. As with any attempt to create a new habit, we won't always get it right. It's taken me five years of failed plans to get to the point where I work out four mornings each week. And I can't tell you how many times Bruce and I were faced with blank stares from our children as we tried to create a family habit of living our faith.

But we kept trying, and we're making progress. Not long ago, Layney was being silly and careless in the kitchen. She caused a big spill right as I was trying to prepare several dishes for a potluck supper. The mess slowed everything down, I lost my temper, and my daughter stomped away, shouting that it wasn't her fault. Because I've known this child for eleven years, I realized her unpleasant reaction meant that she was actually very sorry.

We suffered a few minutes of uncomfortable silence before I remembered something I had recently seen while watching a "Veggie Tales" video as part of our congregation's First Communion class. (Yes, we grown-ups can learn from kids' videos. Remember, we're only as old as we force ourselves to be.) The focus of that class was forgiveness and how important it is to forgive when someone is truly sorry and asks us to forgive. We discussed how badly we feel when we're not forgiven and the joy we feel in knowing that God forgives us all our sins through Jesus.

I went to Layney and reminded her of that video, and I ended by saying the words, "I forgive you." Her thundercloud face turned to a smile, and all was well.

Not twenty minutes later, while I was still frantically preparing the potluck food, Garrett and Kayla were playing too roughly in the next room. Kayla's elbow connected with Garrett's nose, and he didn't appreciate it. He stomped into the kitchen to tattle and get some sympathy, while Kayla insisted repeatedly that it was an accident, that she felt terrible, and that she was very sorry. Hurt and angry, her brother ignored her apologies.

Garrett had witnessed my earlier interaction with Layney, so all I had to say was, "God wants us to forgive people when they're truly sorry." And our son, who has been known to carry a grudge around the world and back, managed to let it go. He forgave his sister, and again all was well. I saw then and there, in the midst of a busy and hectic time, the power of living our faith.

This habit of living faith will continue to grow in our busy family. With practice, the same will be true for your family as well.

It's a day-in, day-out process. Know that there will be times when you fail, when you forget to respond as Christ would have you respond. But together your family will be learning and growing. Through God's grace, you'll always be given another chance.

Blessings to you as you use the simple activities in this book to create a habit of living and active faith in your family—and to have some fun doing it!

ACKNOWLEDGMENTS

Many thanks to my friend and writing partner, Bernadette Stankard, for her encouragement, her inspiration, and her honest critique. I would also like to thank the people of Holy Cross Lutheran Church in Overland Park, Kansas, for their daily ministries and for the opportunity to put many of my ideas into practice. Special thanks, too, to publisher Greg Pierce for taking a chance on a new author, and to my editor, Marcia Broucek, who made this book the best it could be.

ACTIVITIES INDEX BY AGE GROUPS

INFANT & TODDLER (UP TO AGE 3) •••••••••••••
ON THE ROAD

AT THE STORE

CHORE TIME

WHILE YOU WAIT

THE GREAT OUTDOORS

AROUND THE TABLE

BEDTIME

PRESCHOOL (AGES 3-5) ....

ON THE ROAD

AT THE STORE

CHORE TIME

WHILE YOU WAIT

THE GREAT OUTDOORS

AROUND THE TABLE

BEDTIME

ELEMENTARY (AGES 5-10) ....

ON THE ROAD

AT THE STORE

CHORE TIME

WHILE YOU WAIT

THE GREAT OUTDOORS

AROUND THE TABLE

BEDTIME

PRETEEN (AGES 10-12) ....

ON THE ROAD

AT THE STORE

CHORE TIME

WHILE YOU WAIT

THE GREAT OUTDOORS

AROUND THE TABLE

BEDTIME

FOR ALL AGES ••••••••••••••••••••••••••••

ON THE ROAD

BIRTHDAYS

NEW YEAR

LENT/HOLY WEEK/EASTER

BACK TO SCHOOL

THANKSGIVING

CHRISTMAS

TIMES OF SORROW

ACTIVITIES INDEX BY TITLE

A

B

C

D

E

F

G

H

I

J

K

L

M

N

O

P

R

S

T

U

W

Y

Other Resouces for Parents

The Twelve Unbreakable Principles of Parenting
Ann Lang O'Connor

The author wrote this book after she and her husband encountered difficulties with how best to give their children a strong values foundation. They developed twelve core principles to provide a systematic way for them to make decisions on tough issues and day-to-day questions.

112 pages, paperback, $9.95

Love Never Fails
Spiritual Reflections for Dads of All Ages
Patrick T. Reardon

In this collection of reflections, the author celebrates both the joys and the sorrows of parenting. The reflections are accompanied by an inspirational quote from Scripture, contemporary music, or literature, and a link to a website related to the reflection.

96 pages, paperback, $9.95

Moms@MySpiritualGrowth.com
Meditations and Cool Websites for Active Moms

A collection of ninety reflections for moms. Without glossing over the difficulties and stresses of mothering, the author celebrates the spiritual dimensions of being a mom. There is a free website, www.myspiritualgrowth.com, to go along with the book.

96 pages, paperback, $9.95

The Daily Meditations Series

Each book in this series offers 366 days of inspirations that include a daily reflection and Bible verse.

Daily Meditations (with Scripture) for Busy Moms
Patricia Robertson

Daily Meditations (with Scripture) for Busy Dads
Patrick T. Reardon

Daily Meditations (with Scripture) for Busy Grandmas
Theresa Cotter

Daily Meditations (with Scripture) for Busy Parents
Tom McGrath

$9.95, paperback each

Available from booksellers or call 800-397-2282
www.actapublications.com